FAREWELL TO MARRIAGE, LONG LIVE MARRIAGE!

The Shadow of Reality and the Reality of Shadow

MARCEL NGUÉ

Preface by Simon Bolivar Njami-Nwandi

FAREWELL TO MARRIAGE, LONG LIVE MARRIAGE!
The Shadow of Reality and the Reality of Shadow
by MARCEL NGUÉ

Printed in the United States of America
Edited by Xulon Press.

ISBN 9781498468022

While most stories in this book reflect real-life situations, the names and identifying information have been changed to protect the privacy of the individuals involved.

The French version of this book ADIEU LE MARIAGE, VIVE LE MARIAGE! L'ombre de la réalité et la réalité de l'ombre, is also available.

www.xulonpress.com

FAREWELL TO MARRIAGE, LONG LIVE MARRIAGE

The shadow of reality and the reality of shadow

Angingilayé - Éwésé

- Manageable women, but incompetent men?
- Ladies are voicing their opinions: Gentlemen, don't listen!
- Gentlemen are also eager to voice their opinions: Ladies, don't listen!
- Are the standards that are so valued by the world also endorsed in Heaven?
- Why is a precious gift such as marriage so often treated as being of no account?
- It is only during the dry season that the tree is able to spot which leaves are faithful.
- He who disregards the rumblings of thunder will end up being soaked in the rain.
- It is certainly better that you don't vow than to vow and not be able to deliver.
- Money actually has no smell, but life without money can really stink.
- He who wants to keep his friend shall cover his transgressions.
- In most cases, wedding is better prepared than marriage.
- Some very exciting news for unhappy spouses.
- Three main qualities of an ideal spouse.
- God's plan, sexuality and you!
- The marriage quiz.
- Love.

Marcel Ngué

Foreword by Simon Bolivar Njami-Nwandi

Dedication

This book is dedicated to my Dad, Zacharie Ngué, and my Mom, Anna Ngo Balépa. For six decades they were inseparable friends, faithful spouses, and responsible parents. They were blessed with twelve children (six boys and six girls) who gave them forty-five grandchildren and thirty-four great-grandchildren. They live on in the hearts and minds of all who bore witness to the way they still went hand-in-hand together to the market or to church until the end of their lives.

"Entreat me not to leave you,
Or to turn back from following after you;
For wherever you go, I will go;
And wherever you lodge, I will lodge;
Your people shall be my people,
And your God, my God.
Where you die, I will die,
And there will I be buried.
The Lord do so to me, and more also,
If anything but death parts you and me." (Ruth 1:16–17).

Acknowledgments

First and foremost, my special appreciation goes to my dear wife, Madeleine, as well as to our four children, Anne-Estelle, Françoise-Olive, Ivain-Zacharie, and Philippe-Edgar. Like a mirror, they helped me see my imperfections and make constant course corrections. My wish is that this book could be the best legacy I can leave for them.

I am grateful to the authorities of Collège Vogt of Yaoundé who enforced the moral and spiritual education initiated by my Dad. They have collaborated closely, since the 1960s, with their counterpart of Collège de la Retraite, to implement a joint program called "True Friendship". The twinning of these two gender-separated schools aimed at imparting to their students moral purity and respect for the opposite sex.

My gratitude is also due to Family Stations Inc., a Christian organization based in Oakland, California. It was through this institution that I was able to undertake structured training in the Holy Scriptures.

I would like to acknowledge in a special way Daphne W. Ntiri, Professor at Wayne State University for the initial editing of this book; and Ellen Prior for providing a faithful English translation of the original French version of this book.

Special appreciation goes to Simon Bolivar Njami-Nwandi, Professor Emeritus and Dean of the Cameroon pastoral community. Not only did he make significant improvements to the French version of this book, but he also kindly agreed to write the Foreword.

Naturally, the views expressed in this book are those of the author and he alone takes responsibility for them.

Table of Contents

Preface

Farewell to Marriage, Long Live Marriage: the shadow of reality and the reality of shadow is the curious and dialectical title that the author, Marcel Ngué, is using to invite us to read his book. To discuss marriage is to examine the source of human life, of which the sacred union between a man and a woman is the basis. In the author's view, this genetic foundation is established by the Creator Himself. This is why all the inspiration in this book is drawn from the Holy Scriptures. Almost every sentence makes reference to the Word of God, supported by textual quotations. A detailed overview of these biblical passages is provided at the end of the book, so that everybody may be inspired by them!

Farewell to Marriage describes the end of marriage as lived with dignity and endurance by the author's god-fearing parents, whom he takes as his model, an exemplary model of a very large and dynamic family, crowned by a long-lived union of two people.

Telepsép, the book's principal character, deals with marriage issues with authority, like some sort of high priest. Marriage founded on the fear of God has had its day—it is dead! It is dead especially in this 21st century, where the modern world has profaned it by legalizing marriage for all, against all previously accepted standards.

Long Live Marriage is the resurrection of marriage as instituted by God, as it should be lived in sub-Saharan Africa, in connection with the universal tradition of mankind. Until the 21st century, all the people of the earth have remained faithful to the basic principle of marriage based on the union between a man and a woman. This is why the recent intrusion of marriage for all is opposed by the vast majority of the human race. This opposition is simply obeying the inescapable laws of nature, which are obeyed even by animals. The author dedicates all his skills to make this point. He has the means and the will. The son of God-fearing parents, he values the moral and spiritual education he received from his teenage years attending missionary schools, such as the Collège Vogt of Yaoundé. He is a meticulous thinker who is respectful of the ancient sources of our civilization and of the benefits of a good education; hence, his thirst for excellence and for improvement which underpins the wellbeing of Man, created in the image of God.

This wellbeing is founded on the union of a man and a woman, with their indispensable complementarities which form the basis of the family, the fundamental social unit. The author exerts all his literary skill to restore the image of marriage, so that it may live and prosper forever. Hence the noble title: *Farewell to Marriage, Long Live Marriage!*

A faithful and solid marriage! A marriage that is indissoluble and rejects divorce and other forms of deviance. A successful marriage where both spouses stand firm, like a tree which bends in the wind without breaking. In short, a marriage lived in the fear of God. Hence the author's subtle title: *Farewell to Marriage, Long Live Marriage!*

Just as was the custom in the old days, upon the death of a monarch whose line of succession was not in doubt, people would say, "the king is dead, long live the king," *Farewell to Marriage* is, in the context of this book, *the shadow of reality,* while *Long Live Marriage* is *the reality of shadow,* sticking closely to the essence of things in relation to their contingence. The whole philosophy of the book boils down to that.

The target sample covered in the book has been well defined by the author. This can be seen in the characters' names, the places and objects to which he applies his experience as a citizen of the world. Through these interventions, one can sense the influence on the author of his Diasporan experience. Africans living in the Diaspora have a double life, that of their native land and that of their land of adoption. This endows them with a versatile approach. For the author, the Word of God cannot be called into question. Its authority rules the whole world, because it is sovereign and unchanging, based on thousands of years of tradition.

On the whole, this book, which many people can identify with, is highly relevant as it deals with the death and the rebirth of marriage. It is a burning topic which also relates to the political issue of marriage for all! Fighting against that trend, Marcel Ngué's book stands as a bastion and a pillar of resistance against deviant behavior. His teachings on the subject of marriage come at the right time as they remind us of the sacred rules of the only true marriage, which is between a man and a woman, according to God's plan and as consecrated by the laws of nature.

This is a strong message from a man who is firmly convinced that Man was put in this world to follow, over the millennia, the natural laws of creation. Here, the author does well to remind us forcefully that marriage is the pillar and ground of that creation. He does this by referring to one of the most ancient texts of humanity: the Bible, to back up his assertions. As set out in this millennium old tradition, the first human couple was put upon the Earth to tend and cultivate the land, to multiply, to replenish and subdue the Earth. This is how peoples and nations came about. In this context, marriage is the primary living inheritance of humanity. In the modern chaos, where values are abandoned by contemporary society, we must protect marriage as though it were an endangered monument. If this is not done, the marriage institution could be destroyed by predators who are as shameless as they are irrational.

With this firm conviction in mind, I would like to conclude by saying it loud with Marcel Ngué: *Farewell to Marriage, Long Live Marriage!*

Simon Bolivar Njami-Nwandi

Introduction

Do you know any man or woman whose dream is to marry one day? Do you know some who are already married? Are their marriages like smooth flowing rivers, or rather like raging seas? Do you know other people who are divorced or else widowed? And perhaps even some who have remarried? If so, did they at last find the happiness they were seeking? *Farewell to Marriage, Long Live Marriage* is a reminder that marriage, like any other noble project, was never meant to be a pain free experience, nor a permanent honeymoon. It is targeted specifically to all these categories of men and women, whether young or old, rich or poor, with a view to restore their confidence and give them hope, even in a hostile environment or challenging situations.

Biblically speaking (Gen. 2: 18-24), marriage is the very first divinely-inspired social institution, predating the Church and all other forms of government. Not only is it the mother of humanity, but also a foundation stone, the pillar and ground of God's plan. Not by chance does God's Book open with a marriage[1] and close with a marriage[2]. Moreover, the first miracle of the Christian era also took place during a marriage[3]. And, just like all things created by God, marriage between a man and a woman is of incomparable beauty, when each spouse is committed to play his or her role correctly.

Yet, in spite of its beauty and nobility, marriage seems to be losing its appeal. For many young people today, the old adage "getting married is good, not getting married is better" is the way to go. Hence the increasing popularity of cohabitation of unmarried couples, celibacy, divorce, and kids raised by single parents, etc. It is said that if the river has a winding course, it is because there was nobody there to show the straight path. This is not the case for the marriage where guidelines have been around for thousands of years.

The downward slide really began to accelerate in the 1970s, especially after the establishment of no-fault divorce in a number of Western countries. Like a computer virus, these liberal laws have infected God's copyright concerning the institution of

---

1 Genesis 1:27–28; 2:22–24

2 Revelation 19:9

3 John 2:7–9

marriage. Hence, irreconcilable differences, as well as other equally spurious and baseless pretexts, are now considered sufficient grounds for divorce.

Moreover, the feminist movement has driven the nail in even further. Towards the end of the 19th century, its purpose was to remove the social, political, legal, economic, and sociocultural inequality of which women were the victims, and to reestablish their dignity in the society. However, from the late 1960s, the movement shied away from its original goals and began to demand control of women's bodies by women alone—in particular in regards to abortion and contraception—rather than focusing on building a new social relationship between the genders. The man's leadership role was called into question, which triggered a sex war. So much so that nowadays it is difficult to know who is really wearing the pants.

Around the same time, the censorship of movies became merely symbolic, complacent, or even complicit, if it existed at all. This indulgence helped accelerate the general degradation of sex and moral standards, which now threatens the existence of traditional marriage.

Because of this negative trend, the family is generally but a shadow of what it was. It is no longer composed of a respected father, a submissive and honored mother, and humble and obedient children. It is no longer a place where every member of the family feels strengthened by that sense of mutual affection which can heal emotional wounds and overcome setbacks, betrayal, or injustice that might arise. It is no longer a united group whose members pull together, all for one and one for all. It is no longer that haven of peace where an individual can enjoy the incomparable comfort of living among those he loves and who love him in return. And, like a starving ogre, businesses as well as workshops and offices have absorbed a good part of this traditional family, or what is left of it.

Farewell to Marriage, Long Live Marriage examines these changes through the following questions which reflect the multiple challenges faced today by couples in general, and those in sub-Saharan Africa in particular:

- Why do people get married?
- Does God plan and direct all marriage projects?
- Why do married people still feel lonely?
- What is the difference between marriage and partnership?
- Why do the excellent relations that prevail during the engagement period often deteriorate after the marriage has been consummated?

- What does a wife really expect from her husband?
- What does a husband really expect from his wife?
- What are the main causes of infidelity and how can they be avoided?
- How to recover from adultery and its heart-breaking consequences?
- Is Moses' certificate of divorce a carte blanche for divorce?
- Are barrenness, poverty and illness biblical causes for divorce?
- How to survive a divorce?
- Who really benefits from forgiveness?
- Should one remarry his or her ex-spouse?
- How to assess the quality of a marriage?
- What are the three main qualities of an ideal spouse?
- What emotional, moral, and spiritual legacy should parents leave to their children?

The book analyzes these questions and many more using the Word of God, the King James version (KJV) of the Bible, as the blueprint for marriage. The first part of the book, entitled *What Spouses Say and Don't Say about Marriage,* is a series of informal conversations which take stock of the state of marriage today in sub-Saharan Africa. The chapters in this section describe a number of situations which trigger conflicts between spouses. What is uncommon here is the fact that women see the log in their own eyes rather than the speck in the eyes of men. The men also do exactly the same from their side. Through uncompromising self-criticism, *Farewell to Marriage, Long Live Marriage* attempts neither to please nor to displease, but rather to analyze the negative impact of liberal, and sometimes rebellious thinking as the root cause of today's social and family erosion.

The remainder of the book—made up of reports, questions and answers, dialogues and monologues—suggests preventive, curative, and social measures whose aim is to protect the sacred union of a man and a woman. The book is innovative from various points of view: the structured training for spouses; the marriage quiz and its practical use; the profile of the ideal spouse; the unprecedented vow renewal process; concluding remarks revealing the true meaning of marriage; and, above all, the pertinence of the message, which deals with the death and resurrection of marriage, a topic that is generating growing concern and interest.

From beginning to end, the book highlights certain cultural and natural values of sub-Saharan Africa. These include: the great sense of hospitality; family solidarity; the feminine condition; the education of children; the respect for elders; and the connection with the spiritual world.

The main characters are inspired by people of our generation. They are likeable, because they are aware of their own shortcomings and thrive to become better persons. Local names, such as Sabasaba (Saba), Kasimanga (Kasi), Kunyakunya (Kunya), Nléla, or Mpesa, reveal daily living realities which many readers will easily identify with. Words such as *spouse, partner, person,* and the pronouns *he or she,* refer invariably to both men and women.

Another aspect of the originality of *Farewell to Marriage, Long Live Marriage* can be seen in the local toponymy it evokes. As a matter of fact, the names of places in the Mbog Liaa region of Cameroon help explain the text and its setting, and even put certain events into context. Furthermore, footnotes and appendix extend the scope of the message of the book.

Another innovation of this book is the great variety of literary styles used by the author. Like the Bible, the all-time best seller which uses parables or allegories, songs and prayers, *Farewell to Marriage, Long Live Marriage* combines various narrative and descriptive styles including anecdotes and proverbs, swings between poems and poetry, theatre and play, fiction and reality. It alternates between informative and narrative writing. This variety helps to hold the interest and attention of the readers. It also allows them to leave reality momentarily and come back to it, thanks to the joy that procures the decoding of the message.

The expression *Angingilayé,* which appears at the beginning of Part Two, was used in storytelling, especially in the village, by moonlight. *Angingilayé* meant something like: "Hello! May I have your full attention, please?" To which the audience would reply: *Ewésé!* Or *Yésé!:* "Yes, we are listening." This constant interaction between the narrator and his audience helped keep the attention of the listeners alive. Such verbal interaction is used far less nowadays, partly because television has taken over evening time; and also because the tradition of storytelling, whose purpose was to enhance children's comprehension skills and stimulate their imagination, is fading away.

It is our earnest hope that *Farewell to Marriage, Long Live Marriage* will strike a chord with anyone wishing to take a fresh look at marriage in the light of the values and principles laid down by the Creator of this institution.

PART ONE

What Spouses Say and Don't Say about Marriage

CHAPTER 1

Women's Assessment: Don't Listen, Gentlemen

Whenever women get together, they love to talk, mainly about their looks, weight loss, family life, hobbies, etc. Mpesa, owner of Kaba Nyanga Beauty salon[4], and Mbônji, her business partner, greet three of their customers: Nléla, Kétura and Sipora.

MPESA *(After women gave each other big hugs)*: Ladies, welcome to Kaba Nyanga! Looking at you is just like watching a fashion show presenting three models! How on earth do you keep up with your shapes!

---

[4] Kaba Nyanga means "Loincloth and Elegance"

Femininity and the Beauty Industry

NLÉLA: I always eat as much as I want, yet I keep my slim figure. That is 80 percent due to my diet which consists of 25 percent vegetables, 25 percent fruit, 25 percent protein, and 25 percent cereal. The other 20 percent of my weight control is due to sport and aerobic activities. I also go to bed two hours after my last meal, and I get eight hours of sleep every night.

KÉTURA: I avoid staying hungry because hunger stimulates the body to build up stores of fat to replace what is missing. I also avoid all refined foods, in other words, anything where the fibers or nutrients have been removed and replaced by chemical substitutes, either to improve the taste (artificial sugars) or to conserve it for a longer period (salt). These types of foods trigger weight gain and obesity. I also drink hot tea with citronella grass after each meal to minimize the accumulation of fat in my body.

MBÔNJI: So far, my weight control diet has been to limit myself to one meal per day, with only snacks for the rest of the time. Truly, the experiences you have just shared are motivating me to make a radical diet change.

SIPORA: African women aren't meant to be slender. The right curves in the right places are what characterizes our beauty. But once you are in your forties or fifties, it's pointless trying to stay a size 36 or hoping to look like those models you see on the covers of some magazines. Physical beauty is just skin deep. True beauty lies within. It doesn't grow old like physical beauty does. Make-up, massage, plastic surgery, pills and potions, induced vomiting, the use of Botox, manicures, pedicures, and drastic dieting can never defeat the steady effects of "Father Time" and "Mother Nature."

MPESA: We are not only trying to upgrade our well-being and our health, but also to stay in the race, because there's a lot of competition out there. Our husbands mustn't be allowed to think that they married the wrong person. And since a woman's crowning glory is her hair, Kaba Nyanga offers you a wide selection of the top African styles. Whatever the shape of your face or the texture of your hair, thick or silky, rough or fine, the choice is yours. What would you like to talk about during the five hours it will take to do your hair?

NLÉLA: A subject like women's marital woes would help to make the time pass.

MBÔNJI: Women's life expectancy would be interesting too. It is said that we live longer than men, because we spend so much time on shopping and *kongossa*[5].

KÉTURA: How can shopping and sharing secrets possibly affect someone's life expectancy?

MBÔNJI: Apparently, spending money and sharing secrets lower stress levels, just like antibiotics help reduce bacterial infection. It is stress that kills men. But I think the topic Nléla has proposed is the best one.

MPESA: OK! But let's make sure that what is said at Kaba Nyanga stays at Kaba Nyanga. Because only the jar lid should know what's in the jar.

NLÉLA: Motion accepted. Thank you, ladies, for giving me the floor. I've got so many family issues that I don't really know

[5] Relaxed conversation that can cover any subject, chitchat, gossip.

where to start from. The truth is that I am in pursuit of happiness but can't seem to grasp it. I thought my troubles were over when I graduated from school—I had no more late nights, sitting up studying. But that was only one step along the way. Next, I had to find my place in the job market. Then, I thought I could relax when I finally landed a job, because I could buy whatever I wanted. And yet, I still wasn't really satisfied. Because then I wanted, not a boyfriend, but rather a husband who could finally drive away the specter of loneliness and insecurity which never left me.

We Knew How to Organize the Wedding Ceremony, Not the Marriage

The cherry was finally on the cake when I met Makwasi, a well-known athlete. And, only a few months after our first date, we got married in style with all due ceremony and trappings—luxurious and elegant wedding clothes, valuable rings, escorted by best men and maids of honor, colorful surroundings decorated with white flags and multicolor flowers. The music was provided by a famous band and we were entertained by a group of talented comedians. And my hair—it took nearly two days to get it right.

And yet, there were some flies in the ointment even in those early, happy days. This was the proof that we knew how to organize the wedding ceremony, but not how to handle marriage challenges. The following are a few examples of our earliest inconsistencies, shortly after our honeymoon in an exotic, dream location.

Big Boy, can we go to the first screening of the romantic movie that is making the news?

Sweetheart, I'm really not into watching a soppy love story about a couple of nobodies. I'd much rather see something real, like a soccer game or a boxing match.

Big Boy, one of my friends has invited me to her house to help with her hairdressing!

But, Sweetheart, the morning dew only soaks those who are seeking help or a favor![6]

---

6 To reach the house or fields of a distant neighbor, villagers often need to follow a narrow path, overgrown and covered in leaves. The morning dew soaks everyone who passes by. In other words, it is the person who needs a service who should go to meet the person who can provide help. Not the reverse.

Big Boy, I'd like to invite my Mom over for the weekend!

Again, Sweetheart?

Big Boy, maybe I should go back to live with my parents! Because loving someone who doesn't love you back is just like trying to draw water from a stone.

Ngo Kinyok[7], you know perfectly well that nature abhors a vacuum. If you leave, someone else might take your place!

MBÔNJI: Marry in haste, repent at leisure. It's better not to have a date than to date the wrong guy. What on earth made you fall in love with this insensitive and hardhearted Big Boy? He's making your loneliness worse, not only by not approving or offering any alternatives to your requests, but also by systematically opposing whatever could make you happy.

NLÉLA: He was everything that young girls dream of: he was athletic, good-looking, rich, popular, etc. He was a celebrity, a

[7] "Ngo" means "daughter of" in the *Basaa* language. Kinyok is Nléla's father's name. "Ngo Kinyok" means "daughter of Kinyok." When a husband is angry, he doesn't use his wife's first name or nickname (Sweetheart), but rather her maiden name.

dream-guy that all the girls had in their sights. I was proud to be the lucky one that he picked out of so many gorgeous and attractive women. However, judging the book by the cover was my mistake. Truly, people only look good when you have no close connection with them. Cohabitation changes that perception. I remember once, he gave me a check to go Christmas shopping. He looked at me, eyeball to eyeball, and said: "Sweetheart, haven't I given you whatever you wanted? And isn't it right that I also take care of myself?" I did not really understand what he meant. I did notice his absence for the whole weekend. I was in floods of tears, realizing that I had married a mirage. We no longer shared the same bedroom after that. A few weeks later, I was awakened by the offensive presence of someone by my side. He smelled of alcohol. While I was still half asleep, I initiated a strong fight against the offender, shouting out, "Don't touch me! Don't touch me!" Like a ghost, Makwasi slunk off into the darkness, after pulling my left ear.

MBÔNJI: Ah! These men! They behave like a wild bear during the day, but as a lamb at night. They give their wives romantic nicknames with botanical and zoological origins—Honey, Sweetie, Sweetheart, My Watermelon, My Nightingale, My Butterfly, My

Dove—and goodness knows what else! The funny thing is that all these names which imply gentleness and tenderness are a strange contrast to the rough behavior of many husbands.

NLÉLA: Frogs love water, but not when it's boiling hot! And just because frogs don't bite doesn't mean you should put one in your pocket! I was still very young then and the only way I could recover from those early shocks was to go back to my parents. A few days later, Makwasi came by to apologize to his in-laws. Two of his uncles came with him, because only their word would carry weight when dealing with the Nkoña village elders. The visitors were served with *matango*[8] and kola nuts.

All parties brought their wisdom to bear during the palaver[9], drawing on their language skills, their long life experience, their rich repertoire of proverbs, and their sense of humor. Whenever there was a sticking point, the two sides would resort to a time-out, away from each other, to talk it over and come up with a compromise. By doing so, they managed to tear down, one by one, all the walls that were separating them. All ended in agreement and the

8 Palm wine, commonly known as *matango* in Cameroon, is made from the palm tree sap.

9 An African traditional gathering where conflicts within the local community such as poor conjugal and family relationships, adultery, theft, violence, etc., can be peacefully resolved.

in-laws finally departed, with home-grown gifts in their bags. The whole village was happy with this outcome.

SIPORA: This just shows that our sociocultural, ethnic, and religious values run our way of life.

NLÉLA: Absolutely. Later on, my husband's family suffered a loss. The first cousin of the younger sister of the uncle of the grandson of his maternal grandmother dropped dead from a palm tree while he was harvesting palm nuts. The youth association of Mbog Liaa wanted to mark this event with their massive presence. But some associates pointed out that my husband does not usually show up during other families' funerals, even though he sometimes sent money for the occasion. Since physical presence, more than money, was the best sign of solidarity during such occasions, it was decided that my husband should be treated the same way he treats others. There was a general no-show at his household funeral, even though some cash was sent to him. This general boycott taught him a lesson and he no longer failed to attend family events, be they happy or otherwise.

Anyway, I had already forgiven him, because I thought that he had already learned some lessons from all these mishaps.

However, just a few months later, another incident occurred. One morning, Makwasi told me he was going on a business trip. But the following day, he was seen in another part of the town. At first, I brushed this aside as being nothing more than a rumor. But since trust does not exclude control, and to have some peace of mind, I went to visit a friend of mine who lived in that area. The text messages she and my husband exchanged a few days earlier triggered my suspicion. When I got there, I was faced with the reality: my husband had caught the *missionnite*[10] virus. Surprised by my unexpected visit, and anxious to avoid his fun from being spoilt, he did all he could to drive me away. The neighbors did not know what was going on, but they stood there watching.

MBÔNJI: Lies can blossom, but they certainly don't give good fruit. All seems fair in love as in war. Indeed, marriage involves so many dirty tricks, so much cunning and hypocrisy, that it has lost all its appeal. In public, some couples make a show of being loving. But the mask comes off as soon as they get behind closed doors. Truly, if I were you, I would have avoided that type of humiliation by not going there.

---

[10] A created word referring to sexual dalliance on the part of people who go on business trips.

He Who Disregards the Rumblings of Thunder Will End up Being Soaked in the Rain

KÉTURA: A sister ought not to interfere in her brother's private life. But a husband isn't a blood relative. So, it's perfectly normal that his wife should know who he is dealing with, particularly when it is a person of the opposite sex, and furthermore, his wife's personal friend.

MPESA: This shows that we should carefully manage the relationship between our female friends and our husbands, because the closer they get, the easier it is for them to cross the line. I wonder what has happened upon your husband's return from his "business trip!"

NLÉLA: When he came home in the evening, he found that my defensive arsenal was in place—silent treatment, no meals, no eye-contact, and, naturally, no intimacy in the bedroom. That is the way we lived for many months. Then, realizing that to continue living that way made no sense, I finally left. The divorce was pronounced later on with the fault assigned to him. He who disregards the rumblings of thunder will end up being soaked in the rain.

KÉTURA: Some husbands show no respect to themselves, nor to their wives and children. The eighty–twenty code, which means that a man should spend 80 percent of his time with his wife and 20 percent with his mistress, is a disruptive and destabilizing addiction. What wife will be pleased to learn that her husband's commitment to her is only 80 percent?

MBÔNJI: Text messaging is awesome, but it encourages infidelity, because even a shy person can now send or receive secret love messages; and an unfaithful husband or wife would do so in the presence of his or her spouse without raising eyebrows. What is worse is that, even when the mistress is not around, the unfaithful husband keeps thinking about her. So really, it is she who gets the 80 percent! What wife will be pleased to learn that her husband's commitment to her is only 20 percent? Moreover, there are some people who think that a husband who spends time with his wife is unfaithful to his mistress! Anyway, a dog that likes chasing green mambas ends up being bitten.

SIPORA: Ladies, with all due respect, and without playing the devil's advocate, I would like to point out that men can certainly do a lot of things on their own, but they can't activate the eighty–twenty code alone. It could only happen with the active complicity and collaboration of two women—his wife who rejects him, and his mistress who is ready to play the game. So, we are both victims and guilty of what is happening to us. That was just a side comment. Nléla, continue your story.

NLÉLA: When a woman is disappointed in her husband, she usually turns to a man she already knows, so that she doesn't have to start from scratch. This is why I turned towards Misongi, my ex fellow-worker. He was older and less good-looking than Makwasi, but he was more mature and smarter. We got married shortly after. The prospects for this new relationship looked good. Because Misongi really knew how to entertain me with his jokes, and he did it in a way that no one else could. For instance, he would compare me to a luxury car, for which spare parts could be found nowhere; or a star in the sky; or a colorful bauble on a Christmas tree. He would say that when he looked at me time seemed to stand still. As if he were an archeologist, he would say that the more I advanced in age, the more I was attractive to him.

He also knew how to defuse a matrimonial tiff. I remember once when I was very angry he told me to make the best out of a bad job, because men are like snow in the month of March.

KÉTURA: And what does that rather exotic metaphor mean?

NLÉLA: People from the Diaspora often have a different way of expressing themselves, because of their exposure to various cultural influences. Misongi simply meant that I should be patient with him because men's lifespan is usually shorter than women's. It is like snow in the month of March in western countries—it is short-lived because of the rain and the rising temperatures when spring time is near.

SIPORA: I don't buy sweet-talking, because it usually lacks sincerity.

NLÉLA: Verbal or physical abuse is certainly worse! The fact that Misongi is a heavy smoker is what I held against him most, because I'm extremely allergic to strong smells. His smoking addiction made me feel worse when I became pregnant. To justify himself, he told me that according to the latest scientific studies nicotine could have an anorexic effect. In other words, it could regulate appetite, making it very useful to combat weight gain and obesity. *(Sobbing)* I failed to convince him to overcome this addiction, so I had to . . . break up with him.

MPESA: Be courageous, Nléla! You really loved that one!

It's Not That Women Are Hard to Please, It's That Men Are Incompetent

NLÉLA *(After regaining her composure):* What really drove me towards divorce was my spiritual counselor who told me: "Daughter, since your husband doesn't want to change, why would you continue to suffer? God will surely give you a better husband. Just hang out in places where classy people usually go. I promise it won't be long before one of them falls into your arms. Anyway, you have my blessings." One year after the divorce, Misongi called me to tell me he had completed a detoxification treatment and wanted to reconcile with me. I told him, "*Miso,* I care about your health and I have already forgiven you. However, if you really love me, let me enjoy my new life."

SIPORA: With a little bit of patience, you could have saved that marriage. I don't condone those who take sides in a matrimonial dispute, as your spiritual counselor did, without talking to the other spouse. Sometimes, the devil is not as black as he is painted. Anyway, let's listen to the rest of the story.

NLÉLA: A year later, a new suitor, well-off but quite far up in years, proposed marriage to me. His old age was not the main problem; it was the tufts of hair that were growing out of his ears and nostrils, which gave him a rather mystic look. I politely drove him away. A little bit later, a computer professional also made me an offer. I should say that over time I have adjusted my criteria because love has different cycles. At age twenty, I was dreaming of a young, strong, lively, eager man. At age thirty, I wanted a good provider who could help bring up our children. Once I hit forty, I was more interested in a man who is aware that he has one mouth and two ears and is using these two organs proportionately. My new suitor's profile fits the bill, but he didn't get off to an easy start:

- When he first offered, I said, "No! No! No!"
- Two years later, I said, "No! Yes! No!"

- One year after, with some hesitation, I said, "Yes! Yes! No!"
- After six months, I said, "Yes! Yes! Yes!"

MBÔNJI: This is the proof that, for a woman, "no" is not always the final answer, especially where marriage is concerned. It simply means "Not now, perhaps later." All things come to those who wait. Those who want a lasting relationship will have patience. But those who are just looking for fast food will give up. That's how we should sort them out.

NLÉLA: That's right! True love doesn't give in easily. You can chase it away; it will always come running back. Lightning and love leave your clothes intact but would burn your heart to ashes. I thought my third attempt would be the right one, because Saba is quite different from my two ex-husbands. He is a sober and peaceable person. He doesn't drink and he doesn't smoke. He is home-loving and very tidy. Because of all that, I agreed to further lengthen my already extremely long name:

Ngonda Kinyok Makwasi Misongi Sabasaba, Rose Céline, alias Nléla.

But is this really the end of the road? I believe so. The reality is that with a run of bad luck even something soft can hurt you. One day, while Saba had gone to visit his mother at Puma, I sent him the following text message: "Squirrel, I miss you. Be wise and be good. I love you!" His prompt response was: "Ngo Kinyok, that's the first time I hear you talk about love! Could it be that this message came to me by mistake?" His perception triggered suspicion, with all its negative consequences.

MBÔNJI: In western culture, the verb *love* is like breakfast, dinner, and even supper for many spouses. People use it time and again. But in our culture, we prefer to feel love rather than to talk about it. For a bantou woman, for example, fluttering eyelids are enough to express romantic feelings. But our men hardly say "I love you," except when their wives have packed their bags to go to an unknown destination. It's not that women are hard to please, it's just that men are incompetent. Nlela, go on with your story.

NLÉLA: After this text message incident, I and my husband became like two sides of the same coin which, even though they are always together, can never look at each other in the eye. Conflicts were inevitable. Day after day, it was a tug-of-war situation[11]. Our marriage had become like a war zone. Not able to bear it any more, my husband decided to leave, after using rude words. Anyone who kills with the sword, with the sword must he be killed. What goes around comes around. I thought that I would find another suitor on the rebound, just as I had when I was in my thirties or forties. But today, I feel like Siberia—everyone knows where it is, but no one wants to go there.

MPESA: What—Siberia? You are more like Africa, hot and under-explored!

SIPORA: Does a banknote lose its value because it has been ripped?

NLÉLA: All the same, men need to understand that the words they say become their master, while the words they don't say remain their slaves. They ought to know that it's the words they don't say that make them what they should be, and not the words that fly from their tongues. A verbal skid happens easily because our tongues are in a slippery platform. But a word once spoken is past recalling. Words can be used to build and reconcile people.

[11] A tug-of-war is a game, a contest in which two people or teams pull opposite ends of a rope in an attempt to drag the opposition over a central line. It just means here that conflicts between the spouses were permanent.

However, just like a spark, they can also burn the house down. It is the only wild beast that man has not managed to tame. Like a circus lion, words should be kept behind bars so that they don't become hurtful, even harmful. Most successful people major in listening than in talking. Some husbands need a pacifier in their mouth to stop them from hurting their wives' feelings. But is there a mouse so courageous as to put the bell on the cat's collar?

No Woman Gets the Man She Hoped for, and No Husband Hoped for the Woman He Has

MPESA: Speech is silver and silence is golden. But it's not only unkind words that can destroy a marriage. The tendency of some spouses to grow apart can have a worse effect. For my own part, unknown to my husband, I bought a plot of land in the name of my niece and I put up a building there and rented it out. I also opened a bank account abroad in my maiden name. I did all this in preparation for a possible divorce, because one should make hay while the sun shines. When my husband found out about these secret transactions—and I don't know how that happened—he accused me of financial adultery. Divorce was inevitable. But once you've been bitten by a snake, you're afraid of an earthworm, or even a piece of string. That's why transparency is a golden principle in my new marriage.

MBÔNJI: Barrenness is also a source of trouble, and it's always the woman who gets the blame. My mother-in-law was always checking on the shape of my belly beginning only three months after the wedding. Every time I went to the village, I felt her eagle eye on me. She would spy on me from a distance when I went to the river to bathe. After three years, she was convinced of my barrenness and she reminded her son that his responsibility was to ensure the continuation of his lineage. I preferred divorce to the option of polygamy which was proposed to me. In due course, I had two children. Five years after remarrying, however, my ex has yet to become the father of a child. A disappointment can be a blessing in disguise as I now have time to enjoy life. For instance, when I want to buy a dress or a pair of shoes, or when I want to go on a trip, I don't have to consult anyone. I do what I like, when I like, as I like it—with *my* money. All the same, it would be stupid and irresponsible for a married woman to lead such an independent and self-centered lifestyle. One cannot have his cake and eat it too. We have to choose between celibacy and marriage. We can't have it both ways.

MPESA: False friendships can also threaten a couple's unity. For instance, when I was having problems with my ex-husband, one of my clients tried to cheer me up by saying, "I have no patience with men who depend on their wives to top up their wages. I am happy to have divorced in order to marry a rich businessman. Not only does he pamper me, but he shows no interest in my salary. Why should a beautiful and well-educated woman like you waste time on a loser? You can certainly find a more dynamic partner." Advice is cheap. Is a husband like an electronic gadget, something to be replaced when a newer model comes on the market? I learned later on that my counselor was not as happy and as contented as she made out, because her co-wives and their children were constantly at war with her.

NLÉLA: I admit to having made some mistakes. For example, my husband had promised me a nice surprise to celebrate our fifth wedding anniversary. He wanted us to go to a quiet and remote location. Waza, in northern Cameroon, was the ideal place. I loved the idea of visiting the National Park, and I was proud to tell my friends about this project. But when one of them told me she had just come back from Europe, where she and her husband had gone to celebrate their first wedding anniversary, I did all I could to nip the planned trip to Waza in the bud. It was probably the biggest mistake I ever made in my life.

KÉTURA: Life is not a competition. We should never compare ourselves to others. It leads to jealousy, envy, and all sorts of complexes and temptations. The worst part is that we focus all our attention on what others have, without knowing how they got it, nor what else they don't have. By the same token, we complain about what we don't have, without counting our own blessings. If we enjoy what life offers, and do not complain about what life doesn't offer, we are well on the way to success. Needless to say, everyone has different gifts just as every animal, according to the morphological features of its species, has a different way of carrying the baby. For example:

- Mother Monkey carries her baby in her long arms which are fit for the task.
- Mother Kangaroo, who does not have long arms, carries her baby in her pouch.
- Mother Crocodile has no long arms either, but her platform-shaped back allows her to carry her baby.

Like those animals, we have to make the best with whatever gift we have. We need to tailor our needs according to our means, without any inferiority complex.

MPESA: Our husbands deserve a fair and better treatment. We usually play a flute-like symphony when dealing with our kids or our guests. But when we are dealing with our husbands, it is rather military notes that we trumpet out, and their echoes can be heard at a distance. That double-standard is unfair. If a woman is not vulnerable to her husband, to who else can she be, without feeling guilty? No woman gets the man she hoped for, and no husband hoped for the woman he has!

I Am Like a Waistcoat Which, While Having More Buttons than the Jacket, Knows That Its Natural Place Is Underneath the Jacket

SIPORA: Nowadays, women have become very controlling. They say that if the husband is the head, the wife is the neck that can turn the head around at will. We should not change family dynamics by stepping on men's toes. Majôman, for example, used to give instructions, not suggestions, to her husband: "Kurukuru, why hasn't the trash can been emptied yet?"; "Kurukuru, go and pick up my clothes from the dry-cleaners!"; "Kurukuru, why haven't you washed my car?"; "Kurukuru, for heaven's sake—*w*hy are my shoes still lying in the hallway?"; "Kurukuru, do this, Kurukuru, do that, Kurukuru, do it all." It is just like a witch bossing an orphan. Feeling permanently belittled, scorned, humiliated, and even emasculated, Kurukuru decided to keep a low profile in order to avoid daily arguments. He ended up vanishing away, leaving no trace. Personally, I wouldn't wish to be married to a man who, like a snail, shies away when challenged as it would deprive me from the security I am expecting from my husband.

KÉTURA: The hen knows when it is dawn, but she waits for the rooster to crow. If male leadership is being challenged, it's because some men don't initiate anything. They don't have an entrepreneurial mindset and they don't invest enough effort to finish whatever they have started. I certainly don't like Majôman's bossy and controlling style, but I can understand her because, to some extent, Kurukuru reminds me of my husband. The difference is that it is my husband who still wears the pants. I have no intention to compete with him. I do not condone the feminist movement, which emboldens women and softens up men. My role is to be like a waistcoat which, even though it may have more buttons than the jacket, knows that its natural place is underneath the jacket.

MPESA: I would like to seize this opportunity to ask you, "What are the main qualities a woman should look for in a husband?"

NLÉLA: Well, that's a very subjective and very personal matter. Personally, I would expect my husband to be available, because his role is to take care of me and ensure that I don't feel lonely. He should be a good listener. He should be all romantic. It would be a mistake for him to take me for granted, because I am a different woman every day. Why would a man fail to give a woman her due, for instance, in the form of compliments and encouragement? And that's not all I need. I also want a relationship where honesty, loyalty, and fidelity are the key ingredients. When a man really loves his wife, he cannot be a cheater. He cannot humiliate her, or abandon her, let alone be guilty of domestic violence. In case we don't agree on a specific subject, my husband should be able to convince me, with the power of his ideas and character, and not with the power of his vocal cords or his muscles. Better brain than brawn.

MBÔNJI: In fact, a husband should be a good provider as well as a dynamic, committed and caring person. He should also be a visionary. He should know what he wants and do whatever it takes to deliver. He should show proof of sacrificial love towards his wife, be an excellent communicator and find interesting topics to talk about every day. Hence, solitude and monotony would have less impact.

KÉTURA: A trustworthy husband should not just be a baby-maker. He should also be a committed parent. His role is not only to raise his children, but also to help them become the responsible parents of his grandchildren. He should ask God for wisdom to fulfill his role.

MPESA: A recent family survey in a neighboring country has revealed that about 65 percent of women and 40 percent of men are not sexually fulfilled, especially after the third anniversary of their marriage. Even though these statistics may not describe the reality in our country, they reveal the congenital selfishness of men. They need to rethink the way they operate.

Love Is a Flower Which Should Be Watered with Friendship and Humility

SIPORA: What the Word of God is saying about bishops also applies to any respectable man who loves his wife. He "must be blameless, the husband of one wife, vigilant, sober, of good behavior (1 Tim. 3:2)." But a husband can only play his role correctly if his wife is his ally, and not his competitor or rival. Enough said. Let's get back to the subject at hand. Nléla, correct me if I'm wrong, but your husband hasn't yet filed for divorce?

NLÉLA: Not yet, to the best of my knowledge!

SIPORA: Good! No one is perfect, but everybody has at least one good quality. Do you think that this also applies to your husband?

NLÉLA: Absolutely. He's not a hypocrite. He doesn't drink. He doesn't smoke. People trust him and often come to him to seek for his advice. But his words are as sharp as a scalpel.

SIPORA: Focus on the positive points you have just brought up about him and less on his shortfalls. Believe me, many women would like to hang with such a man. Perhaps he is aware that abandoning his wife was a mistake, but pride might be preventing him from making a U-Turn. Encourage him to do so.

KÉTURA: Women have the power to make and break our homes. Did Delilah not melt down the powerful Samson? But we should never follow her wicked example. As a spider secretes silk to spin its web, we should instead weave a web of peace and love over our home, and keep it constantly watered with friendship and humility.

MPESA: Nléla, I wish you would not say to your husband, "No! Yes! No!" Or "Yes! Yes! No!" But rather simply,"Yes! Yes! Yes!"

SIPORA: Ladies, let me tell you a little story before we head home. There was a husband who had done everything in his power to please and be reconciled with his wife; it did not work. One day, as he was driving home from his work, he was involved in a deadly road accident at Matomb village. His car somersaulted nine times before it disappeared in a deep abyss. When the emergency workers finally reached him, all he managed to say was, "Tell my wife I'm gone" (farewell). His wife cried her eyes out when she heard this heartbreaking news, because she realized that it was too late to reconcile with her husband. She is still crying for his loss even today, as she feels closer to him in death. She regularly spends long hours of meditation at his graveside. That widow is here today. She is among us. She is with us. She is talking to you right now. It is me, Sipora. Ladies, don't duplicate my mistake. Be inspired by Mother Theresa's advice, "If we really love, we must learn how to forgive." The sooner the better, as death sets no appointment. God won't ask you how many times your husband hurt your feelings—He knows it better than you—but rather how many times did you forgive him?

NLÉLA: I thank you for your valuable advice, which broke my heart. I can assure you that the seed you just sowed did not fall on rocky soil or among the thorns. I know what I have to do next.

With that said, the women kissed each other good-bye and promised to meet again soon.

CHAPTER 2

Men's Assessment: Don't Listen, Ladies

Kasi, Kunya and Saba, three longtime friends, meet in a convivial corner. Usually, when they get together, they talk more about science, technology, sports, and politics. But this time, they have decided to change the trend by focusing on marriage and family issues.

KUNYA *(To Saba and Kasi):* Hello, my dearest and best friends! It's been quite some time since I have seen you. How is life treating both of you?

SABA: Hi, Brother! I'm still chewing the kola nut[12], and I am still crushing hazelnuts with the palm of my hand[13]. But that's nothing new. Since childhood, I've always managed to cut my way through the undergrowth without a machete[14].

KASI: Hello, my dear friends! Every day comes with breaking news and our ears never go to bed hungry. What breakfast for our ears?

Intelligence Quotient or Emotional Quotient?

KUNYA: The old debate about the age of the Earth is coming back. Some people, referring to the Bible, explain that the earth is about 13,000 years old[15]. Others, referring to the theories of Charles Darwin, Alfred Russel Wallace, and other evolutionist gurus, conclude that the Earth is four to five billion years old. I also read an article that said that with a diameter of about 13,000 kilometers—108 times smaller than that of the Sun—the earth is one of the smallest planets in the solar system. Its distance related

12 I'm still alive.

13 I do whatever I can with limited resources.

14 Been there, done that, since my childhood.

15 Camping, Harold, *Let the Oceans Speak,* Family Stations Inc., Oakland, CA, 1982).

to the heavens corresponds to several million light-years. One light-year, which is the speed of light in empty space, corresponds to ten billion kilometers.

SABA: That would give a distance in the order of ten to a power which even a computer would have trouble in calculating!

KASI: Time out! Dear friends, let's drop this pedantic and ethereal discussion and come back down to Earth. As husbands and fathers, our emotional quotient matters more than our intellectual quotient. After all, our wives want their husbands to be men with heart of flesh and above-average emotional intelligence, rather than insensitive and pedantic scholars.

Love the Woman You Wed, and Don't Wed the Woman You Love

SABA: As far I am concerned, I have to say that my upbringing from childhood wasn't a good preparation for marriage. In fact, after the death of my parents, I was on my own. I filled in my time by picking up girls. All were fish that came to my net. I talked to them sometimes like King Solomon: "You have captivated my heart, my sister, my bride; you have captivated my heart with one glance of your eyes"[16]; and sometimes like Molière: "Of love, fair Marquise, your lovely eyes make me die"; or the other way around: "Your lovely eyes, fair Marquise, die of love, make me."[17] Admiration, curiosity, desire, temptation, the slip, the fall, followed by disappointment and regrets were my journey. I recall that, one day, a girl had to remind me that her eyes were to be found above her nose and not on her bosom, where my wondering glance had landed. I also believed that like illness, love should always lead to bed. While I thought that I was picking up girls, in reality, they are the ones who were seducing me—and self-control was not a virtue of mine.

I came to my senses when one girl offered me a *honoris causa* paternity. Her pregnancy began a few months before I even met her. She knew it. I knew it. We both knew it. But she still went ahead and put that heavy burden on my reputation. Of course, no one believed my denials.

---

16 Song of Solomon 4: 9

17 The Middle-Class Gentleman (*Le Bourgeois gentilhomme*): Fair Marquise, your lovely eyes make me die of love.

KUNYA: This reminds me of the story of Agatha[18]. That's what usually happens to womanizers, Brother. A man doesn't prove his masculinity by messing with girls' affections, but rather by comparing himself to virtuous men, especially those who have managed to create a united and happy family, and have led an exemplary life in spite of the challenges.

SABA: That's right! But it's not how you start out in life that really matters, but what you have achieved in the long run. I am using my past as a springboard, no more as an excuse. Trials and errors, I have to admit, have given me the opportunity to grow. Because I finally came to understand that increasing the number of girlfriends or extending the duration of an engagement, were no guarantee of a happy marriage. The proof—I was engaged to my first wife for a good twelve years, without any major problem. But once we married, my happiness fizzled out. This confirms the fact that women worry about their future *until* they get married, while men worry about their future *from* the day they marry.

18 "Agatha" is one of the fetish tracks by the famous Cameroonian musician, Francis Bebey, in which he sings: "Agatha, don't lie to me, it's not my child (a half-blood), you know it very well. It's not my child, he is yours".

KASI: It is commonly said that love will make you blind, but marriage is an eye opener! Looking back, we can say that our ancestors kept their eyes open on traditional values, some of which—especially those relating to sexual purity before marriage—were in line with what is laid out in the Bible (Lev. 21:13–14; 2 Cor. 11:2). A man's occasional visits to his fiancée were supervised. Cohabitation, premarital sex, or pregnancy were considered dishonorable not only for the girl, but also for her parents and her whole family. Before the wedding, families taught their offspring about how to handle their future marital and parental responsibilities. They made noncommittal inquiries about the personality of the fiancé (e), to see whether he or she will be a good match for their son or daughter. They also conducted a background check targeting the whole potential family-in-law, to see whether the alliance with them would be a worthy one. Different times, different manners—such a scrutiny is no longer enforced today, as most marriages are arranged among young people, often away from their parents and relatives. Many of those marriages have a very short lifespan.

KUNYA: But we must admit that even if our ancestors were less acculturated than we are today, they still had domestic issues. Sure, the world has made great progress in scientific and technological terms, but not on the human level, because, in spite of this progress, families today have to face the same challenges as those of yesteryear. The fundamentals of human lives and the challenges remain practically the same: distant or insensitive husbands, controlling or manipulative wives, disobedient and disrespectful children.

SABA: I am pleased to note that, after all, I am a better person today than I was a few years ago. I have learned that man's first responsibility is to love the woman he weds and not to wed the woman he loves. All that glitters is not gold.

Money Has No Smell, but When You Don't Have Money, Life Really Stinks

KUNYA: Eh! Brother, you're sounding like a real philosopher!

SABA: My successive love setbacks have turned me into a philosopher. It's lucky though that my wife is not around. She would have said that I sound rather like a person who has lost his mind.

KASI: The huge gap between spouses' perceptions can sometimes seem hilarious. And sometimes laughter is the best way to cope with the situation. Not long ago, when I was pruning a tree behind our house, my wife came and said to me, "Cassius, can you guess what today's breaking news is?" I answered offhandedly that in the afternoon the Indomitable Lions of Cameroon would have a friendly soccer encounter with the German national team, the *Nationalmannschaft,* as part of their preparation for the 2014 World Cup in Brazil. "No, Cassius" she insisted, "What I am referring to is more important than soccer. Today is the first of June, you remember?" Seeing that I still didn't get it, she marched off, slamming the door behind her. It was only after she left that it came to my mind that June 1 was actually her birthday. What a blunder, what a gross, stupid, and careless mistake! To control the damage, I went immediately to the market. I brought her a gorgeous, first-class evening dress with stylish women shoes. She sniffed at this lovely gift without, however, actually turning it down. Being aware that a man cannot please a woman without affecting his bank balance, I gave her my credit card. Although this generous move cost me a pretty penny in the space of a few hours, it helped save our relationship. To win a war, one can afford to lose an occasional battle. Anyway, June 1 is now firmly engraved in my memory as an indelible tattoo.

SABA: There is certainly more drama in my love story. Because of my unstable life, I'm more like a rolling stone that gathers no moss, or like a fly searching for some place to land.

KUNYA: Love is like the blade of a sharp knife. It can cut the hand that holds it. How would this apply to your case? In other words, what is the cause of your emotional wounds?

SABA: My conjugal illiteracy is top on the list. I made binding commitment without knowing where I was headed to. My precarious financial situation was also a big factor. In fact, every time I go through a financial dry period, my marriage sinks. No money, no honey. The best way to assess how close the spouses are is to see how far apart they sleep from each other. In my case, the no-man's-land between my wife and me extended from two to thirty inches. It's true that money has no smell, but the reality is that when you don't have money life really stinks. It stinks so badly that your wife and your friends will run away from you. You are just like a hyena whose bad smell has the power to drive away even a lion.

KUNYA: But a friend in need is a friend indeed, and it's during the dry season that the tree knows which leaves are faithful!

SABA: As well as those that are not! I still remember one time when I was going to my bedroom. I didn't know that my wife was right behind the door, which knocked her slightly when I pushed it open. When I was not financially challenged, an apology accompanied by a kiss would have been enough to control the damage. But instead of returning my kiss, she instead landed a heavy slap right in my face. It made me see daytime fireflies. The strangest part of all was that she kept on hitting me, crying out loud, as though it were me who was beating her up.

KUNYA: It is written, "Faithful are the wounds of a friend; but the kisses of an enemy are deceitful (Prov. 27:6)."

Possessing a Woman's Body but Not Her Heart Means Holding an Empty Shell

SABA: Except that the enemy is sometimes on the wrong side. Alerted by her cries, the two young guys who were living with us came up running. Without even trying to understand what was going on, they threw me to the ground and broke my glasses. Realizing that they were part of the problem and not part of the solution, I improvised a defensive move on the carpet which swept both of them away from me, and the fight ended as my aggressors surrendered. My wife needed no better opportunity to confirm her disenchantment in me. She claimed that her life was in danger, because she was sleeping next to a loaded gun; that is, an unpredictable, brutal, and violent man. "My feet and my arms," she said, "were more dangerous than a firearm." She used her deflection skills, her ability to cause the blame to change the direction, to make people believe she was the victim, not the aggressor. Her artificially exaggerated version of events, mixed with tears, convinced even the most skeptical listeners. No one believed my own version.

KUNYA: A crying woman will always get away with her offenses, because people will naturally sympathize with her. You can't beat that. But it seems that it is your own son, and not the younger brother of the half-brother of the nephew of the aunt of your paternal uncle, who threw you to the *tatami!*[19]

SABA: He does not know the difference between a living room and a *dojo*.[20] Fortunately, he doesn't look like me. He took after

[19] The mat used for the practice of Japanese martial arts. It completely covers the floor of the dōjō and is softer than the traditional flooring.

[20] The place where martial arts are practiced.

his mother. Like mother, like son! A week after this sad incident, I discovered upon returning home that my house had been literally emptied of its contents. I had known for a long time that my wife was planning to leave and she was just waiting for an opportunity to justify her move. She finally got it. The fact that this incident took place the same day she got the keys to her new house tells the whole story. Apart from my library and my wardrobe, she spared virtually nothing, not even the dishes, the carpets, and the curtains which I had bought before our marriage. I slept on the floor that night. Everything I had accumulated over the years was all gone in one day. Possessing a woman's body but not her heart means holding an empty shell. It only increases the loneliness syndrome that marriage is supposed to cure.

KUNYA: I have noticed that when our wives are around, we complain about them, and even when they are absent, we still talk about them. How is that?

SABA: Can you spend time talking about somebody who is not important? On my ex-wife's initiative, we were divorced a few years later. But when I finally got a decent job, she wanted to come back. She was in love with the money, not with me. But when a hunter is right in front of a hare and he cannot gun it down, what chance does he have to hit it when it is speeding away? I have already turned the page and I was dating a physiotherapist. She caught my attention not because she was good-looking—and she surely was—nor because she was from a rich family, while I was from a family which was also rich—but in debts. She caught my attention because, unlike the other women on my short list, she was fond of reading the Scriptures. I told myself that this was exactly the type of person I needed in order to grow up both morally and spiritually.

But my better half was very controlling. She wanted to check up on everything I was doing, as though we were in a police state or a nursery school. Often, I let her get away with it, because any objection or any challenge on my part usually triggered a severe retaliation. It is said that whoever has the gold makes the rules. But this golden principle is irrelevant in marriage—whether poor or rich, I am THE MAN! This has more to do with God-ordained roles and responsibilities than anything else. My wife wouldn't buy that. Irreconcilable differences was the argument she used as a *deus ex machina,* after only eighteen months of marriage. As we went our separate ways in the hallway of the court, she told me, "Saba, it isn't really your fault. I'm used to living alone and taking care of myself. I'll continue to do just that. Bye-bye!" As the saying goes, easy come, easy go.

KASI: For many couples, mine included, incompatibility can sometimes be more real than compatibility. For example, I am curious and interested in almost everything, while very few things excite my wife, except perhaps if she learned one day that the sun had risen from the west or the Atlantic Ocean is flowing to the Sanaga or the Wouri rivers. I like discussing about how to solve problems, while she likes talking about her feelings and her emotions. I am very untidy, but she is very disciplined and orderly. I like to spend and she likes to save. But even if we are different in a thousand ways, there is one thing that is keeping us together—the fear of God. That is why we are like two opposites which keep attracting each other. We respect our differences, because without these, our relationship would be so gloomy and dull.

KUNYA: The expression *irreconcilable differences* is generally used by those who want a divorce. It is nothing but a prevarication, a pretext to disguise their inability to love and be loved, a subterfuge to be free and do whatever pleases them. But let's turn that page. What about your third wife?

SABA: Brother! Never tell the river, "River, I would drink your waters no more." After dancing the bafia dance[21] with my two ex-wives, I really didn't want to marry again. But something unexpected made me change my mind. When the uncle of the son of my niece passed away, his friends and acquaintances came to his funeral with many wreaths. But the deceased had no dependents. He was both an orphan and the only child from his parents, and he had just divorced. Not knowing what to do with all the wreaths that they brought, his friends simply hung them on the branches of the trees. I got the message in a very powerful way. That is why I soon found myself once more on the treadmill with a new wife. The first year, I spoke and she listened. The second year, she spoke and I listened. But the third year, we both spoke and our neighbors listened. To avoid further escalation of the conflict, I finally decided to rent an apartment. Desperate times, desperate measures.

KASI: When you want to save a dying tree, you have to cut out all the affected part right down to the root of the problem. Then

[21] This is the traditional dance of the Bafia people, in the Mbam region of Cameroon. It is one of the most elegant dances of the country. It involves taking two steps forward and one backwards. This led to the expression "to do the bafia dance," or, in other words, to find oneself in a situation which is difficult to resolve.

you medicate and irrigate the tree. Have you applied a similar treatment to your marriage?

A Woman Is as Difficult to Understand as the Bible, Even When You Have Studied It

SABA: I really did everything in my power to identify the root of the problem. I also approached other people to get some advice from them.

- Some of my friends told me, "If the temperature is too high, just break the thermometer. Divorce is even the best thing that could happen to you, as you could romance a younger and sexier woman."
- My lawyer set various options before me, all leading one way or the other to divorce court.
- My family, which had snubbed this marriage from the very start, just provided a temporary moral relief.
- My in-laws were also full of advice. But, since blood is thicker than water, they assigned me all the blame, while my wife came out of it with the highest grades and the congratulations of the jury. So, instead of slapping the left

leg where the mosquito had bitten, my in-laws slapped the right one instead[22].

- Thinking that she was blameless, in spite of her own failings, my sweet wife told me, “In the light of your numerous shortcomings that have been pointed out by everyone, don’t you see that *you* need to change?”
- A religious leader listened to me attentively. But instead of comforting me with a prayer or a Bible verse, he said to me, “I see that you don’t love your wife and she doesn’t love you either.” But was it not the reason I desperately needed some help? He gave me the business card of a psychiatrist.

I didn’t set up an appointment with the psychiatrist, because I had no desire to listen to whimsical hypotheses such as: “hallucinations,” “bipolar disorder,” “psychosis,” “paranoia,” “schizophrenia,” or some other pieces of complete nonsense. Do psychoanalysis or neuroscience have anything to do in this case?

- Finally, some of my relatives advised me to consult a certain *Bikolobitja,* a powerful local seer. In my culture,

[22] They were off-topic.

the invisible world controls everything in the visible world. But an invisible world that doesn't refer back to the Almighty God is pretty scary. The scare-merchants make their living by frightening the timid, by presenting huge problems without recommending practical solutions. Forgiveness and reconciliation are nowhere to be found in their prescriptions, only retaliation and destruction. That is why people who consult them always end up breaking up their alliance.

In the end, I decided not to trust anyone else's advice because, for most people, divorce and remarriage are standard prescriptions.

KUNYA: But many of those who take that route don't seem to have peace of mind. Regrets usually assail them. In fact, divorce is a very painful choice, because it wipes out many years of personal and family history. And there is no way to rewrite it. I would like to make a comment about the seers, those people who predict what will happen in the future. I learned that one of them told a young couple who was expecting a baby, "Future parents, I have good news for you—your child will be either a boy or a girl!" How amazing! Would the parents have actually expected something else?

SABA: Maybe a bisexual child, or a hermaphrodite, why not?

KASI: I'd like to say a word or two about in-laws who usually blindly support their daughter. They usually do so when they know that she is able to take care of herself and her loved ones. Even a divorce, in that case, wouldn't bother them. But a marriage purely based on material interests is built on sand. That reminds me of that woman in my village who, like many women of her generation, did not have the privilege to go to school. When a suitor came to ask her father for her hand, she first wanted to know whether that man had a high school diploma!

SABA: She was really modest. She could have even inquired whether that man has a bachelor's degree or even a PhD, why not?

KUNYA: But what was she really looking for, a degree or a husband?

KASI: Probably both and very likely in that same order. But when her suitor learned about her inquiry a few days later, he wrote to her the following: "The decision to break up belongs to the person who makes the call first. So before you reject me, I already did it. Bye!" It's really not a big deal if the relationship breaks up at this early stage.

KUNYA: My grandpa used to tell me that women are as hard to understand as the Bible, even if you have studied it. Even archeologists and psychologists can't grasp the way women think and operate. The more you study a woman, the more you realize that you don't really know that much about her. Because she is like money: if you are handling it carelessly, it will end up making someone else happy. She is like okra sauce: if you don't know how to eat it with your hands, it will slip between your fingers. She is like cassava cuttings which can take root in whatever soil they are planted. She is also like salt which, if not used sparingly, ends up messing up the sauce, and even your life. Lastly, a woman is like math—any inattention or distraction will make 1 + 1 become 3—so much so that I often don't feel qualified enough when dealing with my wife. I don't know how to navigate through her fluctuating emotions. To top it all, she does not share her feelings, but she expects me to read her mind. What wouldn't she tell me how she feels so that I should know what to do?

KASI: Brother, what you just said has triggered something in my mind: What qualities would we like to find in our wives?

SABA: The man's role is threefold: To be a leader (Eph. 5:23); a provider (1 Tim. 5:8); and a protector (1 Pet. 3:7). To succeed in this complex mission, I would need a reliable wife, a sparring partner who, even if we don't agree on certain things, can help build up a strong family. Both of us should be like teeth which, through movements in opposition of phase, work together to break down food and crush it into smaller pieces to feed the same body.

KUNYA: We don't choose our parents, our brothers, our sisters, or our children, and we don't agree with them about everything. But we still love them very dearly. Why wouldn't we extend that love to the women we freely choose to be our lifetime partners? The mistake we make is that, unlike a businessman who selects his partners based on their abilities, we generally choose our wives based on their looks. A man's wish is to have a wife who is outspoken and not secretive, frank and not hypocritical. Moreover, she should be a forgiver, because without forgiveness, cohabitation of two imperfect persons would become a very stressful experience. A smiling wife would also make the difference. I don't mean a fixed grin or a phony smile like the one on the face of the dummy in a shop window, but a smile expressing joy, vulnerability, trust, love, and grace. Such a smile highlights the woman's natural beauty and charisma better than any make-up does.

KASI: In addition to being respectful (Eph. 5:33), the wife should fully integrate her husband in her life, keeping him informed of whatever is going on in her life. She should also support him (Eph. 5:22–24), because she is a valuable helpmate to her husband (Gen. 2: 18).

Life has become so complex that a man can no longer do it alone. He needs a capable woman, like the one who is portrayed by the Dean of Cameroonian pastors. What he is saying about the qualities of the pastor's wife applies to any woman who wants to be a good helpmate to her husband:

"She should be discreet, helpful, hospitable and generous. She should bear herself humbly and modestly, firm so as to avoid creating chaos and complacency in her home. Nowadays, she should be educated and well-informed and have a respectable and lucrative professional life which can make a substantial financial contribution to her household. She should take a close interest in what her husband is doing and provide the support he needs to overcome daily challenges. Only a responsible and capable wife can create the necessary conditions for her family's growth and stability"[23].

In other words, the security a woman is seeking in her marriage also depends upon her capacity to maintain a certain standard of living should something serious happen to her husband. But we, as men, should also embody the qualities we are looking for in our wives. There should be a good match between the two spouses.

My Wife's Ability Matches Her Weakness

SABA: My wife's character is above average, I would say, but having a strong connection, a good chemistry between us is not yet a reality. The stumbling block is that her ability matches her weakness.

KASI: What do you mean by that?

SABA: She has a "phonographic" memory with no scratch in it that could cause her "vinyl record" to skip a groove. Her ability

[23] Njami-Nwandi, Simon Bolivar: "The Pastor's wife" in the Treatise on pastoral ethics, CLE Publishing, Yaoundé, 2005 (pp. 77–82).

to remember my mistakes, no matter how old and how small, is really amazing.

KUNYA: There are no roses without thorns, nor good wood without ants. But every cloud has a silver lining. Your wife's strong points should be a prism through which you should look at her. Cast a veil over her imperfections. Above all, tell her you are sorry for leaving her. Even if you think your share of the blame is only 0.1 percent, act as though you were 100 percent wrong. Don't adopt a defensive attitude. Humbly accept your wrong doings in order to win her heart back. That's what I do to defuse an argument with my angel Mpesa. Just recently, I offered her a weekend at Kribi, a city near the Atlantic Ocean, to evaluate our marriage and recharge our batteries. This trip created unprecedented conditions for dialogue and reconciliation.

KASI: He who wants the honey should cope with the bees. Facing challenges with the winner's mindset. Therefore, when you meet your wife, don't talk down to her like a technocrat or an emperor, but like a vulnerable husband; better still, like a loyal and loving friend. To do this, you need to master the love language she understands best. You could, for example, use these words that I used not so long ago to calm down the anger of my wife Kétura: "*My Queen,* forgive me for the pain I needlessly caused you. Give me a second chance. Even if you have fallen out of love with me, allow me to partake in your healing process." A humble attitude and nice words like these would very likely trigger a positive feedback from your wife. Even if she spurns them, don't give up. With women, "patience and length of time will accomplish more than rage and strength"[24].

SABA: Brothers, I heard you. I thank you for your pertinent pieces of advice. If it has to be, it's up to me.

The three friends promised to keep in touch as each of them headed home.

[24] Jean La Fontaine's fable entitled *The Lion and Rat*.

CHAPTER 3

Youngsters: Better Safe than Sorry!

To help bring about reconciliation between Saba and Nléla, their friends planned to invite them to an event. Deborah (Dédé), head of the Human Resources Department at the University of Kodong, and Sipora's former classmate, offered them the opportunity to attend an Open House at the university campus.

The purpose of this event was to inform students, parents, and teachers about the various opportunities that are available on the job market. Various representatives of the public and private sectors were the main speakers, including physicians, nurses, businessmen and women, army officers, leaders of non-governmental organizations, and many others.

While this information session was going on, Telepsép[25] was waiting for the students at one of the entrances to the campus. He had a megaphone in his hand and a poster which read, "Moral purity is lifesaving." His wait wasn't too long, as the students came surging across the campus to hear what this intruder had to say.

TELEPSÉP: Ladies and gentlemen, you have just been informed about the relationship between school education and the job market. While successful academic or professional achievements are key in your life, moral and spiritual values are critical ingredients[26] that you cannot afford to do without. Unfortunately, the culture we live in today ignore those values. I am here today to warn you specifically against the prevailing idea that sex is what should define who you are. Today's culture would have you believe that virginity is old-fashioned, and that cohabitation cements love. This rebellious agenda will poison your spirit. Ladies and gentlemen, do you realize that God gave you the gift of sexuality for your own good, and not for your destruction? Your body should

25 A moral and spiritual leader. His name means "righteousness" in the Basaa language.

26 *Les jeunes s'interrogent. Réponses pratiques,* Watch Tower and Tract Society of New York, International Bible Students Association, Brooklyn. New York, 1989.

not be an object of pleasure. Therefore, before getting involved in any sexual activity, ask yourself the following questions[27]:

- How should I manage my sex life to avoid mortgaging my future?
- Does premarital sex bring me real and sustainable happiness?
- Does it pave the way for a happy marriage?
- Will it bring happiness to the children who could be born from that relationship?
- Isn't pornography a deadly poison for my spirit?
- Does God condone casual sexual intimacy, with no long-term bonding?

A STUDENT: "Mr. Catechist," can't you find a better job?

TELEPSÉP: Is inviting people to be responsible custodians of their bodies, as recommended by God (1 Cor. 6:19–20), not one of the best jobs there is out there?

[27] This portion is largely inspired by a pamphlet of an anonymous spiritual counselor entitled *God, sex and you*, Yaoundé, Cameroun.

A STUDENT: Sir, we are in the 21st century, but it seems that you are still in the Stone Age or Cave Man Age!

TELEPSÉP: God's teachings are immutable and permanent throughout the ages. The reality is that casual sex provides real—but temporary—pleasure. It has lifetime and eternal consequences, because "He who sins against the Lord shall receive the wages of sin" (Num. 32:23; Rom. 6:23). The wages of sin come in two parts:

- The wage advances
- The full payment

The wage advances are the painful experience that girls who end up with an unwanted pregnancy go through. The child who is born will suffer psychological trauma, because his parents are not married and do not live together. He will also likely suffer from the absence of sufficient material means, because parents who don't have steady work generally don't have the means to take care of a baby. This situation is at the origin of high infant mortality rate.

Young lady, your studies may be interrupted early if you become pregnant. Also, you may not find yourself a husband because most men, even though they are part of the problem, wouldn't like to marry a single mom. Young lady, do you really want to fall victim to godless and lawless sexual predators? So dress decently and not in a vulgar fashion. Clothing that promotes indecent exposure only attracts men of questionable morals. Men with good ethics will likely pass you by. You certainly deserve better. Reserve your sexual purity for your future husband.

Abortion is another mistake that some young girls fall into. This crime is so serious that it will stay with you throughout the rest of your life. You could even be left barren, leading to an unhappy marriage, polygamy, or even divorce.

As for you, gentleman, you ought to treat each person of the opposite sex with respect, and not simply as an object of pleasure. You could end up with AIDS, or other sexually transmitted diseases (STDs), which would ruin your health and your finances (Prov. 6:29). You may also contaminate other partners, even your spouse and your children. Gentleman, do you really want to be a STD carrier?

As for the full payment of the wages of sin, it will take effect on the Day of Judgment (1 Cor. 6:9–10). And that day is coming. Make no mistake about it.

A FOOTBALLER: My football skills attract hordes of female admirers. Do you mean I should turn my back against them?

TELEPSÉP: Will you also be able to take care of the children who might be born from these relationships?

A STUDENT: "Mr. Disciple," if you really care about us, why don't you give us condoms? *(The students begin chanting.)* Condoms! Condoms! Condoms!

TELEPSÉP: You will enjoy life better, not in becoming slaves of your testosterone, but in developing a strong character which is your best protection.

A STUDENT: "Mr. Legalistic Champion," after all, aren't we just human beings, not angels?

TELEPSÉP: Legalism focuses on human laws, ceremonial laws, external appearances, and not on the transformation of hearts. It is this last aspect that I am more interested in. You are absolutely right in saying that we are not angels. But it was to men, in flesh and blood, like you and me, not to angels, that God gave His Testament of love which has the power of transforming hearts.

A STUDENT: God surely wants me to enjoy life. Is there a problem if I have an affair with a girl that I love so dearly and she loves me back?

TELEPSÉP: Lust is not love and two wrongs won't make it right, do they?

A FEMALE STUDENT: "Mr. Apostle," could it be that you are simply jealous?

TELEPSÉP: Jealous of whom? Of a person who is stepping onto a minefield without a guide or who is dancing in a sinking boat?

A STUDENT: "Mr. Moralist," do you want us to believe that you have never been unfaithful to your wife? See you in Hell!

TELEPSÉP: I'll intercede for those who have chosen to knock on the wrong door.

A FEMALE STUDENT: "Mr. Born Again," is the university campus a monastery or a convent for nuns?

TELEPSÉP: Absolutely not, but your campus is part of an institution that strives for excellence and good behavior. *Mens sana in corpore sano*—a sound mind in a sound body.

A STUDENT: But is it wise to buy a pair of shoes without trying them out first?

TELEPSÉP: The tree is known by its fruit. If premarital sex were a guarantee for a successful marriage, would the divorce rate in our society be so high?

A FEMALE STUDENT: Being responsible for yourself is a full time job; why would you moonlight as a judge for others?

TELEPSÉP: My authority, if any, only comes from the Word of God. It is written: "Judge not, that ye be not judged (Matt.

7:1)." To judge, however, does not mean to condemn, for only God may condemn the guilty and reward the innocent (2 Chron. 6:22). However, each and every believer has the moral duty to challenge other fellow believers with respect and love, reminding them what is right (Luke 12:57) in line with God's expectations. It's just like a soccer player reminding his teammates what the rules of the game are, without substituting himself to the referee.

A STUDENT: "Mr. Theologian," I belong to my generation more than to that of my elders. Personally, I will follow your advice only when I reach your age.

TELEPSÉP: Procrastination is not a smart choice, as we know neither the day nor the hour.

A FEMALE STUDENT: Marriage has become so scary that I would prefer to stay single.

TELEPSÉP: Just like marriage, celibacy is a noble option, as long as it is not used as a pathway to immorality. Healthy celibacy makes it possible to better serve God (1 Cor. 7:32–34).

A STUDENT: "Mr. Chaplain," if our moral standards have deteriorated, isn't it the fault of those who removed ethics and religious education from our school curriculum?

TELEPSÉP: First of all, let me say that you can give me all the nicknames you want, and I must compliment you all on your power of imagination. Concerning the point about the absence of religion among school subjects, I fully agree with you on that. But is there anybody among you who might not know the difference between right and wrong? *(Three students shyly raise their hands.)* Those who just raised their hands, while hiding behind their friends, know perfectly well that they are playing the fool. The culture we live in today tolerates casual sex. This addictive trend makes people believe that they are free to use their body any way they want. The following analogy teaches that freedom is not free. A dad left his brand-new car in the custody of his son. Upon his return, he discovers that his *jewel* has been reduced to a wreck—the hood is dented, the doors bent, the bumpers twisted out of shape, and the interior stinks of cigarettes. Would that dad be happy with what he sees? You got my point. You are just the custodians of your body. Will the Owner of your body be happy when He finds out that the beautiful body He gave you was treated as a doormat? Think about that one. I would like to conclude by saying this: "Train up a child in the way he should go: and when he is old, he will not depart from it (Prov. 22:6)." May God richly bless you!

After these words, Telepsép left the campus, to the sound of whistling from some of the students and loud applause from others.

Even though they kept a good distance between them during the Campus Open House and follow-up activities, Saba and Nléla never found themselves so close to each other since their five-year separation. Saba seized this opportunity to have a confidential talk with Telepsép. After giving him some pieces of advice, Telepsép invited him to the forthcoming seminar on family and relationships development. He told him that if he and his wife are finding it difficult to resolve some issues, they shouldn't be ashamed to ask for assistance. He strongly recommended that both of them attend the seminar. If only one of them goes through the healing process, the risk of reinfection would be inevitable. Saba agreed immediately with that offer, but it took a lot of time and patience to convince Nléla to do the same.

PART TWO

Good Bye to the Past, Hello to the Present, and Welcome to the Future!

CHAPTER 4

Angingilayé!

BISSIP *(After a short prayer)*: Ladies and Gentlemen, in the name of VILMA Association[28], I am pleased to welcome you to the Boonjok Family Development Center. Our mission is to give a wake-up call to husbands and wives whose marriage is on the brink of separation or divorce. But even couples who are navigating through smooth seas are warned and equipped to face challenges when they arise. Prevention is better than cure. Hence, the theme of the seminar: *Relationship Development and the Family*. Unexpected changes usually occur when people with similar conjugal experiences meet. It creates an irresistible synergy, a paradigm shift for most of the participants. We hope that, this time around, the same causes would produce the same effects.

---

[28] VILMA stands for *Vive le Mariage* (Long live Marriage).

For our agenda we will listen to six speakers over the next forty-eight hours—three each day. After each plenary session, there will be a breakout meeting—women will meet in the Putkak Room, and men in the Boumyébél Room. On one hand, these breakout meetings are intended to facilitate free and open discussions among people having the same sensitivity; and on the other hand, to allow the working groups to come up with questions which will be addressed in the plenary. Anonymity will be fully respected.

I would like to start off with the story concerning the rebirth of the eagle. ***Angingilayé?***

THE AUDIENCE: ***Éwésé!***

BISSIP: Once upon a time, there was an eagle which lived on the Kingok Mountain, in the village of Somapan. Well-sheltered in his nest on the rocky cliffside of this high mountain, he could survey his territory. His powerful talons, his great hooked beak, and his tapered wings enabled him to soar the skies easily and to attack and capture his prey—rabbits, squirrels, large snakes, young goats, and other small, farmyard animals. His clear and acute vision could pinpoint his prey more than two kilometers away. But for several months, the villagers had not seen the eagle. They thought that he must have gone into exile or perhaps had died. ***Angingilayé?***

THE AUDIENCE: ***Éwésé!***

BISSIP: But the eagle is the longest-living bird in the world. It can live for seventy years or more. In order to reach that age, however, he must take certain precautions. Because from the age of forty, he will start losing his vitality. His sharp and pointed beak and his huge talons begin to curve forwards and he can no longer grasp his prey. His great wings grow more feathers which weigh him down in flight. Consequently, he can no longer use his agility, his speed, and his talons for hunting. ***Angingilayé?***

THE AUDIENCE: ***Éwésé!***

BISSIP: When the eagle found himself at that downwards trend, he decided to retreat from the village skies. He had two choices: do nothing and fade away gradually; or follow a rebirth agenda and start a new life. The second option was his choice. One hundred and fifty days spent alone on the summit of Kingok gave him time to rejuvenate, to go through a painful but life-saving experience. The first thing he did was to get rid of his old, crooked beak that had become useless. He began to knock it off, bashing it night and day against the hard rock of Kingok.

Then Bissip began chanting rhythmically, making knocking sounds: *Bikokibiyoko! Lipémba! Bikokibiyoko! Lipémba!*

Some of the participants joined him in singing and dancing.

BISSIP: *Bikokibiyoko!*

IN CHORUS: *Lipémba!*

BISSIP: *Bikoki-biyoko!*

IN CHORUS: *Lipémba!*

BISSIP: ***Angingilayé?***

IN CHORUS: ***Éwésé!***

BISSIP: The eagle's perseverance paid off and at last the beak broke off. He then waited until his wound was healed and a new beak had grown before continuing with his "plastic surgery." The second phase involved using the new beak like a scalpel to draw out his inwardly curved talons.

BISSIP *(still following the rhythm): Bikokibiyoko!*

IN CHORUS: *Lipémba!*

BISSIP: *Bikokibiyoko!*

IN CHORUS: *Lipémba!*

BISSIP: *Bikoki-biyoko!*

IN CHORUS: *Lipémba!*

BISSIP: ***Angingilayé?***

IN CHORUS: ***Éwésé!***

BISSIP: Again the eagle waited for these new wounds to heal and for new talons to grow before beginning the third and final phase of his rejuvenation process. This basically involved trimming his over-feathered wings, to allow him to fly more easily.

BISSIP *[Still with the same rhythm]: Bikokibiyoko!*

IN CHORUS: *Lipémba!*

BISSIP: *Bikokibiyoko!*

IN CHORUS: *Lipémba!*

BISSIP: *Bikoki-biyoko!*

IN CHORUS: *Lipémba!*

BISSIP: *[Loudly]* ***Aaangi-ngilayéé?***

IN CHORUS: ***Éwé-séé!***

BISSIP: After 150 days, the eagle was once again agile, speedy, powerful, and able to dominate the skies of Somapan. This story teaches us, among other things, that sometimes we have to step back in order to jump higher; we need to look back over our lives, make necessary adjustments and then start off anew; we have to shake off old habits and prepare for a better future. That's the central message of this seminar.

After this appetizer, we will now move on to the main dish, which will be served by a team of experienced men and women. They bring with them a track record of almost 200 years. They have been through thick and thin in their own marriages. Their victories are a beam of hope for those whose marriage is going through a bumpy patch.

The honor of cutting the symbolic ribbon goes to our Spiritual Leader, Telepsép, who requires no further introduction.

CHAPTER 5

When the Divine Copyright Is the Blueprint for Marriage!

—∞—

TELEPSÉP: The pyramids and the calendar are to Egypt what the compass is to China, vaccines to Louis Pasteur, the helicopter to Leonardo da Vinci, and the cell phone to Martin Cooper. Honor should be paid to whom honor is due. Everyone admires the genius of the world's great inventors. But when it comes to marriage, do we also dedicate front page honors to the Creator of that institution? Are God's fundamental principles the blue print through which everything relating to marriage is interpreted?

Marriage, as it is recognized by all governments and cultures, has a unique and special status. It represents the ultimate expression of love and commitment between the husband and the wife. No other relationship on earth can provide that kind of security.

Nowadays however, liberal theories and opinions, which are devaluing biblical marriage, are trying to impose themselves as truth. They call into question the basic principles of a true marriage, defining it on the grounds of rights, needs, selfish pursuit of pleasure, and not as an opportunity to merge and integrate the lives of two persons.

1. A misconception of marriage

For some people, in fact, marriage is seen as a stage in life which brings pleasure and a certain amount of prosperity, while creating a haven of peace where happiness reigns permanently. This egocentric daydream, however, contains the seeds of disappointment.

1) Pleasure

Pleasure is an essential ingredient of any marital relationship, as confirmed by this verse.

"May your fountain be blessed, and may you rejoice in the wife of your youth: A loving doe, a graceful deer—may her breasts satisfy you always, may you ever be intoxicated with her love" (Prov. 5:18–19).

Joy reaches its climax when it leads to procreation. As Yves Nicol explains it, "In Africa, marriage is undertaken specifically with the aim of procreating, so as to ensure the continuation of the clan and the family"[29].

Gwa Cikala Mulago shares the same line of thought: "African marriage is the source of life," he affirms, "the husband is first and foremost a father (or father-to-be) and the wife, a mother (or mother-to-be) of their children. Thus, in an African marriage, the father-mother role takes precedence over the husband-wife role. The woman and her husband only become true spouses when their first child is born, especially the first boy"[30].

---

[29] Yves Nicol: *The Bakoko Tribe* (Larose colonial and oriental bookshop), Paris, 1929. It is cited by Charles Bafinamene in *La stérilité du couple: Approche théologique et pastorale en milieu ecclésial négro-africain.* Masters thesis in Theology, Bangui Faculty of Evangelic Theology, Central African Republic, September, 2009 (pp.85–86).

[30] Gwa Cikala Mulago in *Étude monographique des Bakongo, Mongo, Baluba et Bashi du Congo (DRC), ainsi que les Banyaruanda* (p.67). The preference for "a male child" has its roots in the patriarchal system, the most widespread in Africa. His study is cited by Bafinamene Kisolokele: Ibid. (p.39).

Spouses feel even more fulfilled when they are not just baby-makers, but responsible parents capable of raising their children and giving them a good academic, moral, and spiritual education.

Nevertheless, in spite of its sociocultural relevance, procreation does not in itself make a marriage. Because people do not have to marry in order to procreate. Unmarried people do procreate; so do animals. Therefore, procreation does not, in itself, define marriage and it does not provide a special status before God. Any marriage, with or without children, is considered a sacred union. On the other hand, barrenness is not a biblical cause for divorce.

God blessed Adam and Eve, and told them, "Be fruitful and multiply; fill the earth and subdue it (Gen. 1:28)." This verse does not define marriage. Rather, it evokes the duties and responsibilities attached to the life of a couple. The multiplication here is the consequence and not the cause of a marriage.

2) Prosperity

Prosperity[31] is another key objective most couples have in mind. In rural areas, it is measured by the amount of human and

[31] Hill, Napoleon, *Think & Grow Rich*, (The Ballantine Publishing Group, 1983)

material resources a farmer has. Those resources are the basis for any development strategy[32]. In urban areas, having money makes life easier as it can help acquire all kinds of goods and services.

However, in spite of its importance, money cannot solve all the problems. For example, money can:

- Buy a house, but not a home.
- Buy a car, but not family unity.
- Buy a degree, but not knowledge.
- Boost a savings account, without making provisions for eternal life.
- Buy clothes, but not the garments of salvation.
- Pay for vacation to exotic locations, without providing a permanent cure for loneliness which affects even those who, like Adam, live in an earthly paradise.

People who don't have money complain about their hardship. But even those who are financially in a more fortunate or prosperous condition are worried because they are not sure about what the future has in store for them (Proverbs 23: 5). They have

---

[32] Stanislas Melone *: La parenté et la terre dans la stratégie du développement. L'expérience camerounaise: étude critique*, Yaoundé, University of Cameroon, Paris, Klinesieck, 1972.

no guarantee that they will never lose their assets. The excessive importance and priority given to money and its relentless search has two main side effects: (1) it leaves little room for the spouses to work on their marriage; and (2) to develop a personal relationship with God. The following verse says it all:

> "For the love of money is the root of all evil: which while some coveted after, they have erred from the faith, charity and goodness and pierced themselves through with many sorrows" (1 Tim. 6:10).

There should be, therefore, something more in life than money and all it can buy.

3) Peace

Peace is the third objective married people are usually looking for. They think that peace is possible when everything is going their way. The material needs are met, the wife is respectful to her husband, the husband loves his wife dearly and is a good provider, the children are obedient, and everybody in the family enjoys good health. There is neither challenge nor adversity whatsoever.

But such a peace, if it exists, is very volatile. It is short-lived, because it is built on shaky ground. Anything, a job loss, an illness, even a slip of the tongue can drive that peace away. It happened when a wife asked her husband: "Honey, who is that lady you were talking with on the phone a few minutes ago?" Visibly embarrassed by this question, the husband replied: "You should not count the teeth in the mouth of an adult. After all, I am King-Kong,[33] I AM THE MAN and I cannot be accountable to a woman." But at night, the almighty King-Kong, found himself on his knees, begging for a peace negotiation.

The idea that marriage can be defined by the selfish pursuit of pleasure, prosperity and peace, has destabilized and is destabilizing many marriages, because these ingredients, no matter how important they are, do not guarantee real and sustainable happiness. They promote self-fulfillment, pride, and unfaithfulness, instead of self-denial and selflessness and humility.

This explains why many spouses do not cling to each other and cannot lead an integrated life. They feel sad, isolated, rejected, friendless, forlorn, and lonely.

---

[33] King Kong is a fictional monster. The image of this giant gorilla, holding a young girl in one hand and facing up to an attack by airplanes at the top of a skyscraper, is ingrained into popular culture.

Feelings of loneliness have a negative impact on health and can even lead to stroke or premature death. And, as a risk factor, it is twice as dangerous as obesity and as toxic as smoking fifteen cigarettes a day[34]. The person who suffers from loneliness falls easily into the trap of picking just anyone as a friend. A lonely person is, therefore, more vulnerable to temptations. It is usually the case, especially for spouses who choose to lead separate lives. Reconciliation becomes difficult, if not impossible, when either embarks on a new romance with somebody else.

God's blueprint teaches what true marriage looks like.

2. The original design of marriage is better than its corrupted copy

In God's economy, marriage is not about the pursuit of material possessions, prosperity and peace, but about how spouses can drive away solitude by becoming *one flesh*. This is what the following verses teach:

> "It is not good for the man to be alone. I will make a helper suitable for him" (Gen. 2: 18).

[34] *Réveillez-vous!* Avril 2015 (pp. 10-11). D'après une analyse de 148 études par des chercheurs.

"Therefore a man leaves his father and mother and clings [or cleaves] to his wife, and they become one flesh" (Gen. 2:24).

Two heads are better than one. With this kind of marriage, each spouse tries to understand the intimate, emotional and spiritual side of the other. They build trust and confidence in each other. They stick together, work together and celebrate life together, till death separates them. Divorce, therefore, is not an option.[35]

The following five analogies are an illustration of what marriage looks like in the spiritual realm.

1) Marriage and omelet
2) Marriage and painting
3) Marriage and organ transplant
4) Marriage and magnetic fields
5) Marriage and lichen

1) Marriage and omelet

When you prepare an omelet or scrambled eggs, you mix eggs, salt, and other ingredients. Overbeating toughens the proteins in

35 Mal. 2:16; Matt. 19:8

the white. Once the mixture is ready, the white and the yolk of the eggs can no longer be separated. Loyalty is the name of the game.

The same goes for marriage. It seals the destiny of the husband and the wife (1 Cor. 11:11–12) who have become one flesh. The indivisibility of the couple is protected by the Creator of that institution.

This sacrosanct principle is reinforced in the following four analogies.

2) Marriage and painting

In painting, when you mix two primary colors, you obtain an indelible secondary color. For example:

Yellow + red = orange;
Red + blue = purple;
Blue + yellow = green.

Once mixed, the two primary constituents can no longer be separated, even with a solvent or chromatographic paper. It is impossible to dissociate yellow from red, red from blue, or blue from yellow, once the secondary colors (orange, purple and green, respectively) have been obtained.

The same goes for marriage. It is intended to create an unbreakable and indissoluble bond between a man and a woman (Gen. 2: 24).

3) Marriage and organ transplant

Organ transplant is the surgical removal of an organ from one person and its transplantation into the same person or another person. This procedure, which brings together the components from the donor and those from the recipient, is lifesaving and gives the recipient a wonderful new lease on life.

The same goes for marriage through which the husband and the wife become one flesh. Their ethical and spiritual markers agree because the husband and the wife have identical tissue-types (Gen. 2:21–24; 1 Cor. 11:11–12). The wife's body belongs to her husband and the husband's body belongs to his wife (1 Cor. 7:4).

To avoid potential risks of repulsion or rejection by the spouses and have a sustainable marriage, the husband should love his wife, even if she does not deserve it; and the wife should respect her husband, even if he does not deserve it. Because true marriage is about grace and not merit.

4) Marriage and magnetic fields

Becoming *one flesh* can also bring to mind the magnetic field created when two magnets are rubbed against each other and placed side by side. They attract each other's iron-containing objects. By so doing, they produce a magnetic field external to both of them. Identical poles (north-north or south-south) repel each other, while opposite poles (north-south) attract each other. The two opposite poles stick to each other to form a single, large magnet with one single north pole and one single south pole.

This is what marriage is supposed to accomplish: the husband and the wife are attracted to each other like magnets to experience the beautiful mystery of love and life[36].

5) Marriage and lichen

Lichen is a complex organism made of both a microscopic aquatic algae and a filamented fungus. The relationship between these organisms has real advantages for both of them. It is a mutual relationship, and not a commensal or parasitic one. The algae nourishes the fungus which, in turn, provides the water and

[36] Jean-Benoît Casterman: *Pour réussir ta vie sentimentale et sexuelle, À toi qui veux aimer et être aimé(e)*, SOPECAM, Yaoundé, January, 2011.

carbon dioxide which the algae needs for its photosynthesis. They are interdependent because each one ensures the survival of the other. They form an indivisible entity.

The same goes for marriage. It should be a cross-fertilizing and mutual edification process. Because the husband and the wife are called upon to form one flesh, to live for each other, until death separates them (Rom. 7:2; 1 Cor. 7:39).

Although it is not a husband-wife relationship, the bond between Ruth and her mother-in-law Naomi is an example of loyalty which should inspire all spouses. She told her mother-in-law:

> "Where you go I will go, and where you stay I will stay. Your people will be my people and your God my God. Where you die I will die, and there I will be buried. May the Lord deal with me, be it ever so severely, if any but death separates you and me!" (Ruth 1:16–17)

These two verses teach that the power of love should be greater than the risk of separation (Matt. 19:5).

Like Cain (Gen. 4:9), each spouse is accountable to God and must be prepared to answer the following question: "Husband, where is your sister?" Or: "Wife, where is your brother?" This is because the husband and the wife are the closest of brothers and sisters. Therefore, each of them should play the role of a watchman for the other (Ezek. 33:6) by caring, interceding for each other, and helping each other to feel loved, accepted, protected, and above all, less lonely.

* * *

*

Why Are Relations Between a Man and a Woman Generally Good during the Engagement Period, Only to Deteriorate after They Are Married?

There are many reasons that could help explain why it is so.

1. The belief that marriage is just like any business partnership
2. The lack of adequate marriage preparation
3. The money *factor*
4. Premarital sex
5. The belief that a happy marriage is just a matter of luck
6. The impact of what spouses say or don't say
7. Being sick and tired of doing the same things over and over

8. External factors: false friends and true enemies
9. The lack of eternal vision

1. The belief that marriage is just like any business partnership

As it is commonly said, partnership is a business entity which can have multiple partners. It has a provision for its dissolution and the release of the parties from their duties, for example, in case of bankruptcy, or if there is a change in the business climate or individual goals. A clean break will then give peace of mind to all of the parties, discharging any remaining obligations and concluding the arrangement amicably. Parties are free to create new partnerships with new people.

Marriage is a totally different ball game. It is the highest expression of love and loyalty between one man and one woman. It is a lifetime covenant. As a covenant, and contrary to the partnership provisions, marriage requires that, should one spouse become insolvent for any reason (accident, illness, job loss, etc.), the other should do whatever it takes to bail him out responsibly, instead of growing apart. That's the beauty of marriage. Competition or rivalry, abandonment or divorce, are no biblical options, but rather the outgrowth of man's wickedness (Matt. 19:8–9). In God's economy, once married, always married.

> "So they [husband and wife] are no longer two, but one flesh. What therefore God has joined together, let no man separate [put asunder]" (Matt. 19:6).

Only death can bring marriage to an end (Rom. 7: 2), for the simple reason that the purpose for which the marriage was contracted can no longer be upheld. That is what the following verse teaches.

> "A woman is bound to her husband as long as he lives. But if her husband dies, she is free to marry anyone she wishes, only in the Lord" (1 Cor. 7:39).

Marriage is going through the most critical period of its history, because the world is treating it just like a partnership that can be dissolved for any reason.

2. Lack of Adequate Marriage Preparation

Marriage is one of the few professions which people undertake with no training nor experience whatsoever. It is as if human DNA contains genetic information predisposing men and women to naturally play their marital roles correctly. But it is not so. Nobody can play a piano or drive a car without learning how to do it. And marriage is much more difficult to master.

Many decades ago, some churches offered marriage preparation internship. The preparation sometimes lasted one full year. Today, however, such opportunities are rare. When one is available, it only lasts a few hours, sometimes with no follow up. And many people cannot afford to pay the enrollment and training fees.

Consequently, most people marry without fully knowing what they are getting themselves into. After the demystification period, which usually lasts two to three years, some spouses, especially those who consider that marriage is just a partnership or a stop along the way, and not a final destination, do not hesitate to call it quits. Those who stay the course endure their marriage instead of enjoying it.

3. The Money Factor

Money is a servant, not a master. It is a tool that provides the ability to maintain or improve the standard of living of the family and, eventually, to help others out (gifts). The more money one has, the more choices he can afford. He can choose what to eat, what car to drive, what college his children should go to, what type of vacation his family should have, etc. Money also helps connect frequently with friends, for example, in hosting periodic parties and get-togethers.

However, many family surveys have come up with the same conclusion: Money is the marriage breaker number one. Many spouses are, indeed, constantly stressed out about money. Its absence or mismanagement triggers frustrations, stress, envy, conflicts and resentment. It is also at the origin of many cases of adultery, separation or divorce. The vow to be and stay married in wealth as well as in poverty is not binding for people who think that no money, no honey.

To have a successful marriage, the relationship between the spouses should be stronger than the love of money.

4. Premarital Sex

Lust, which often manifests itself from the earliest encounters between a man and a woman, muddies the waters and gives rise to false hopes. Moreover, cohabitation or premarital sex does not guarantee that the marriage will be a successful one.

The following analogy shows how premarital sex is counterproductive. A blood test, for instance, requires that the patient remain without food for at least eight hours before testing for blood sugar levels, for maximum sensibility to insulin. To eat within that time frame would not produce reliable lab results.

By the same token, it would be ideal, even though difficult in the culture we leave in today, to abstain from sex during the engagement period. Such abstinence helps conduct a dispassionate and non-complacent study of the personality and character of the future spouse.

5. The Belief that a Happy Marriage is just a Matter of Luck.

People who have not been successful in marriage think that a happy marriage is just a matter of luck. That would mean that successes as well as failures are only due to good luck! If it were so, nobody would be accountable for the way he handles his marriage. Getting lucky is not the same as becoming successful. Spouses won't be truly fulfilled unless they feel a genuine sense of consistent achievement. The difference between a hunter and a farmer is a good illustration. The hunter reaps without sowing, as he does not raise the animal he is aiming at. He just comes across it and guns it down. But the next day, he will likely go home empty-handed and unhappy, because every day is a new dawn. The farmer, on the other hand, knows that success is 1 percent luck and 99 percent perspiration. Therefore, he minors on luck, but majors on the sweat of his brow: He has to clear land of overgrowth and undergrowth, sow, water and fertilize the soil, etc. He knows that he can only reap if he performs his diligent responsibilities.

The same goes for spouses who do not wish to leave their future to chance. They know that marriage is not like a peaceful walk in a park, nor like a cruise trip during which travelers are taken care of. Rather, marriage is a training ground where the spouses must navigate through obstacles and challenges in order to acquire the qualities that define love. Among these are:

patience, perseverance, endurance, self-control, faithfulness, humility, loyalty, empathy, altruism, and the like.

Spouses should behave like farmers, and not like hunters.

6. The Impact of what Spouses Say or Don't Say

What the spouses say reveals who they are, as well as the level of their moral and spiritual maturity. To strive for excellence, husbands and wives should complement each other whenever one of them is planting good seeds in the other, in words as well as in deeds. If a criticism is to be made in order to upgrade a spouse's performance, it should be formulated in a loving way. A convenient time and moment where the two spouses feel very close to each other will help convey the message more efficiently.

If there is nothing positive to share, it is better to keep quiet, as "out of the same mouth should not come forth blessing and cursing" (James 3: 10). What is said can make or break up a marriage.

7. Being Sick and Tired of Doing the Same Things over and over

A battery loses its energy as it keeps being used. The same goes for marriage: Monotony, boredom and internal conflicts between the spouses usually cause lots of wear and tear on their relationship.

To jump start their relationship, each of them should look at the log that is in his own eyes and not the speck in the eye of the other. They should evaluate their individual performance with a view to reversing the negative trends and bringing new habits into play. Where there is a will, there is a way.

8. External Factors: False Friends and True Enemies

People who are closely related to a fiancé usually tell him certain truths about his future mate, in order to help him understand what he is getting into. But once the marriage contract has been signed, spouses should protect themselves against any negative and divisive influence. They need people who can help them overcome their challenges, and not those who would become part of the problem.

But choosing people who can have a positive influence on the couple can sometimes be a very painful decision to take, as it implies giving up on some longtime friends. The best friends are those who recommend forgiveness and reconciliation, and not those who promote the separation and divorce agenda. Tell me who your best five friends are and I'll tell you who you are.

9. The lack of vision

The lack of vision affects all that has been said earlier. Spouses spend so much time complaining about each other that they finally destroy their most precious asset. Each of them believes that he is putting more into the relationship than the other. Each of them ignores or devalues whatever the other spouse has done or is doing for his family, in terms of physical presence, security, leadership, advice, financial contribution, the moral and spiritual education of the kids, prayers, etc. Each of them complains about lapses in each other's role: the husband is not a good provider, and the wife is not a respectful partner, and so on. But God put them together so that they could bring to light each other's weaknesses with a view to correct them and build each other up. He put them together so that they could become reliable sparring partners. He put them together so that they could help each other walk by grace and not by merit and, by so doing, to bring them closer to His own image. God's purpose is greater than temporary possessions and pleasures.

Spouses are only aware of the importance of marriage after they have lost it, or after one of them has died. "Where there is no vision, the people perish" (Prov. 29:18). Save your marriage, no matter how challenging it may be. Challenges teach you how to cope with difficult situations, how to build your character and become a better person. Above all, they teach you how to grow in faith.

* * *

*

Adultery and abandonment are biblical causes for divorce. Yet God is against divorce. How can these two conflicting points be reconciled?

It is true that some Bible verses state that one may divorce in the event of adultery (Matt. 19:9), or abandonment (1 Cor. 7:15). But other verses teach that God hates both adultery (Heb 13:4) and divorce (Mal. 2:16). Repentance, forgiveness, and reconciliation are God's way (1 Cor. 7:11).

The following verse teaches that God would like each marriage to be healed:

> "And unto the married I command, yet not I, but the Lord, Let not the wife depart from her husband: But and if she depart, let her remain unmarried, or be reconciled to her husband: and let not the husband put away his wife." (1 Cor. 7:10–11).

Unlike a rental agreement or a business partnership, the rights conferred through marriage are inalienable. They cannot be revoked or transferred to a third party on any pretext whatsoever. The marriage covenant contains no provisions for dissolution, nor any clause for modification of its terms and conditions.

Can an offense as serious as adultery be forgiven?

There is a difference between forgetting, forgiving, reconciling and rebuilding trust. Forgetting is a biological function. Everything that happens throughout our lives is, so to speak, chemically or electronically recorded in our subconscious mind. However, the pain caused by adultery may diminish in the long run, especially if the offending spouse truly repents and changes gears. However, an offense as serious as adultery can never be forgotten. But it could be forgiven.

Forgiveness, on the other hand, is a spiritual function, a graceful act which consists in never reminding either the offender or anyone else of what happened. It smothers and fights off this bad memory every time it tries to emerge. It rises above the offense in order to save the relationship of the two spouses. It is a painful experience which can only achieve anything if the victim puts himself in the place of the offender with a view to understand his motivation. The couple should decide whether professional assistance is needed to help them heal the emotional wound one of them may have inflicted on the other. The guilty spouse should be forgiven, not because he deserves it, but because forgiveness is about grace, not about merit. Vengeance and retribution belong to God (Deut. 32:35), and nobody gets away with sin (Nu. 32: 23).

In fact, forgiveness does greater good to the person who forgives, because repaying evil with good (1 Pet. 3:9) enables the forgiver to recover his peace of mind. To forgive is, therefore, like setting a prisoner free, and that prisoner is the person who shakes off and moves on.

While forgiveness is a painful step to take, reconciliation is a special blessing (Matt. 5:9). Forgiveness is the graceful act of *one* spouse who decides to render good for evil, while reconciliation is the initiative of *both* spouses, who are committed to work together, with or without the assistance of a counselor, to make things right again.

The rebuilding of trust is a very slow process that could lead to a new start. Spouses decide to count on each other again, regardless of what may have happened in the past, in order to build a better future. They give themselves a second chance.

Should we forgive, even if the offender fails to repent?

A conflict between spouses can be compared to a car breakdown. Some minor problems, such as a broken light or a flat tire, can be easily identified and fixed by the driver himself. However, other, more serious problems such as starter failure, or the engine or the transmission breaking down, require the intervention of a mechanic who can diagnose the problem, whether mechanical or electrical, before he can get it fixed. In case of a structural problem, for example, defective tires or airbags, fixing the problem will require the expertise of an engineer or a product designer.

The same goes for marriage. Couples should determine the level of expertise that might be required to help them overcome their differences. The seriousness of a conflict depends upon the perception of the person who is abused or cheated on. If the victim considers the offense benign, forgiveness should be granted, with or without the repentance or confession of the guilty party. But if the victim considers that the fault is a very damaging one, she should confront the offender with factual evidence if possible in order to bring the truth to light. She should explain how the offense has negatively affected her reputation, her job, her relationship with others, and with God. One of these two things may happen. If the offender repents, he should be forgiven (Matt. 18:15; Luke 17:3–4). He should be told, however, that forgiveness is not a license to do the same thing again.

But if the offender minimizes the offense, or if he simply denies everything and even refuses to repent, the spouse who is betrayed should still forgive. Forgiveness is a grace, not a merit. However, in this case, the victim should not inform the offender that he has been forgiven, because the guilty party may believe that it is possible to get away with an offense without the slightest repentance. In this case, the assistance of a trusted counselor may be required (Matt. 18: 15–17), a counselor who shares God's wisdom and not his personal opinions or those of the world.

When two spouses do no longer love each other, isn't it better that they separate in order to avoid further escalation of the conflict?

Separation could be an option if it could effectively help avoid further escalation of the conflict. In this case, it should be temporary (a few weeks or months) so as to not expose the spouses to temptations (1 Cor. 7:5). It would, therefore, be highly recommended, during the separation, that both spouses follow a structured training program with a view to help them become a better husband or a better wife. A separation without a joint improvement program is counterproductive, as the same problems will likely pop up if the spouses get back together again.

When the separation takes too long (more than six months), it usually restores old habits or creates new addictions which will delay or even jeopardize the reconciliation process.

Since the New Testament era, we are under God's grace. Do we still have to apply the letter of the law when dealing with divorce or remarriage?

To determine the path to take, many people rely on academic freedom. For such people, there are no moral absolutes, and it is up to them to determine what is right and what is wrong. This leads to confusing interpretations on the subject of divorce and remarriage. Too many cooks spoil the broth.

Many others rely on man-made laws, as was the case with the legalistic Pharisees (Matt. 15:2–3), or on human traditions (Matt. 15: 2–3). Others believe that God's mercy will spare even those who tempt Him (Luke 4:12), by rejecting God's standards and standardizing man's way.[37] For sure, God is Love, but He is also Justice, and His laws have teeth[38].

On the other hand, there are people who religiously follow God's instructions. They do not seek to modernize His laws, nor to soften or reform them. Because all that God has done is perfect, and nobody can improve on that. They consider that the practices contained in the Old Testament are the New Testament guiding

[37] To paraphrase the philosopher Hubert Mono Ndzana: "Écarter la norme et normaliser l'écart," *Interview sur les voleurs à col blanc, Camer.be, Cameroun & Société, 2013.*

[38] Nu.32:23; Joh. 12:48.

principles and precepts. Are lying, stealing, killing, adultery and homosexuality, for example, still serious sins today? You bet!

BISSIP: Mr. Telepsép, we thank you for your powerful message that shows where we usually slide before the fall occurs. We should stay true to the blue print of biblical marriage. We should protect it as the African Organization for Intellectual Property (OAPI) protects writers' copyrights. Patriarch Bisohoñ will now explain how to navigate through marriage fluctuating waves.

CHAPTER 6

A Marriage That Is Not Challenging Cannot Edify

BISOHOÑ: My name is Bisohoñ *bi* Bandôn; Bandôn *ba* Mpeg; Mpeg *mi* Njéé; Njéé *i* Ten; Ten *i* Hot; Hot *i* Gwel; Gwel *i* Bisu; Bisu *bi* Yede; Yede *i* Wél; Wél *i* Nkoo; Nkoo *u* Banomok; Banomog *ba* Nguu; Nguu *i* Bôt; Bôt *ba* Nnanga; Nnanga *u* Njob; Njob *i* Nlénd. I come from Boonjok (Nkoña), Puma Mboglen, Kamerun. This is how the genealogy of a Basaa from the sacred territory of *Mbog Liaa* is presented.

For your information, I am only eighty-one, and my sweetheart Anna is only seventy-six. My wife is a blessing. She respects me, even if from time to time I forget the way to the bathroom. I don't believe that any other woman could have coped with my many imperfections for over six decades. By the way, we celebrated our diamond wedding just a year ago.

A few years ago, the air conditioning (AC) system in my car got messed up. I took it to a garage. The mechanic requested and got my commitment that I will pay the bill no matter what the nature of the problem, the cost of the spare parts and the labor.

It is in this manner that marital issues should be handled. Spouses should commit to face any problems, any obstacles, any hardship, regardless of their nature and their scope. The cohabitation of two persons with different personalities and backgrounds naturally triggers internal conflicts and contradictions. Spouses should stay the course no matter what comes their way.

Marriage is an investment in love which generates interests and dividends, if both spouses are willing and committed to build a strong relationship and to learn, among other things:

1. How to deal with financial issues
2. How to deal with sexual intimacy issues
3. How to deal with communication issues
4. How to deal with spiritual disharmony
5. How to deal with child-raising issues

6. How to deal with in-laws
7. How to deal with domestic violence

1. How to Deal with Financial Issues

As a good servant, but a bad master, money has ruined the lives, dreams, careers, reputation, and the legacy of many people. As confirmed by many social studies, money-related issues are the principal cause of marital crises. The situation is usually explosive when the husband, the head of household, is financially challenged (job loss, illness, retirement). While supporting and encouraging her husband to stay strong during this painful experience,[39] the wife should act as a brave copilot and do whatever is legitimate to avoid a family crash. Insolvency is not a biblical cause for divorce.

Financial hardship is by no means the only cause of an unsettled household. There can also be lack of transparency in the way financial resources are handled during the accumulation, the preservation and the distribution phases.

Careful budgeting and good resource management, based on the following three principles which are endorsed by millions of

[39] Njami-Nwandi, Ibid. pp.77–82.

people across the globe, are essential. Couples could be inspired by these principles in doing whatever it takes:

1) To save regularly
2) To borrow wisely
3) To repay promptly

1) To save regularly

Whatever amount of money is put aside on a regular basis will accumulate like drops of water from a tap. Emergencies, tuition fees, retirement, new economic opportunities, and other short-term and long-term investments, can fully or partially be covered with personal savings. Given their importance, savings should not be what is left over after all other budget items have been covered, but rather the first expense,[40] the first item that should be secured.

As shown in the two following examples, it is not how much money somebody earns which matters, but rather how much can he set aside for himself.

---

40 Mintzer, Rich & Kathi: *The Everything Money Book. Learn How to Manage, Budget, Save, and Invest Your Money So There's Plenty Left Over*. (Holbrook, MA: Adams Media Corporation, 1999).

Example 1:

Nestor and Rosalind make $10,000 per month, but their household expenses amount to $13,500. So, every month they have a shortfall of $3,500, which is $42,000 annually. They live hand-to-mouth, without a safety net. To balance their budget and save some money, they need to either find a way to increase their income, or to make drastic budget cuts, downgrade their lifestyle by limiting their expenses to real necessities. They should focus on their basic *needs* and not on their *wants* which could easily become a bottomless pit.

Example 2:

Victor and Solange make $5,000 per month. Their bills amount to $4.500. They are able to set aside $500 per month, which is $6,000 annually. They know how to take care of the pennies and the dollars take care of themselves. This couple is better off than the first one, because their savings will provide some protection during rainy days.

Experience shows that those who know how to balance a budget (income and expenses), and how to save and invest their hard-earned money, will likely have a better retirement. They will likely be less dependent upon their families, their friends and their government.

2) To borrow wisely

Being *a budgeter* is better than being *a debtor*[41]. A budgeter avoids being in debt. He carefully tracks his spending, documenting any expense that has been incurred on a daily basis. He relies on his savings and avoids, to the extent possible, spending the money he does not have (credit). His debt, if any, is generally a *good debt,* as it is invested in essential goods, mortgage, college education, or a business that can generate profit and eventually pay back the debt. He does not borrow to buy luxury items, fancy cars, bigger TVs, expensive clothing and jewelry, vacations in exotic locations, etc.

Each couple should determine how much they can borrow.

3) To repay promptly

People usually borrow from a family member, a friend, a financial institution, a bank, a credit union, or a tontine. The

[41] Mintzer, Rich and Kathy: Ibid.

payment can be made in one lump sum at a lower interest rate, if the borrower can afford it; or gradually at a higher interest rate. It only becomes an issue when the borrower is unable to pay off the debt, with accruing interest, within the commonly agreed timeframe. He who pays his debts grows rich, while he who accumulates debts gets poorer. To avoid being "the slave of his lender (Prov. 22:7)," the borrower should carefully analyze his purchasing power before he accepts the deal.

The take away here is Solomon's wisdom:

> "[God] Remove far from me vanity and lies: give me neither poverty nor riches; feed me with food convenient for me: Lest I be full, and deny thee, and say, Who is the LORD? Or lest I be poor, and steal, and take the name of my God in vain." (Prov. 30:8–9).

2. How to Deal with Sexual Intimacy Issues

Sexuality is the most intoxicating, the most hypnotic, the most absorbing, and the sweetest of life's experiences, as we read in this verse:

> "Let thy fountain be blessed: and rejoice with the wife of thy youth. Let her be as the loving hind and pleasant roe; let her breasts satisfy thee at all times; and be thou ravished always with her love." (Prov. 5:18–19).

Sexuality is the gift of love, God's blessing to couples:

> "Let the husband render unto the wife due benevolence: and likewise also the wife unto the husband. The wife hath not power of her own body, but the husband: and likewise also the husband hath not power of his own body, but the wife." (1 Cor. 7:3-4).

Sexuality allows couples to fully celebrate their union, to get regularly connected to each other and, eventually, to have children and create a family (Gen. 9:7). More than anything else, sexual intimacy is a special moment when husband and wife can feel closer to each other, and realize that each truly belongs to the other (1 Cor. 7:4).

However, sexuality is often the first fuse that blows up when spouses have an argument. For men a conflict can sometimes be like an aphrodisiac; for women, however, a conflict usually leads to a mental block that can last for several days, several weeks, several months, or even several years. And yet God commands:

> "Defraud ye not one the other, except it be with consent for a time, that ye may give yourselves to fasting and prayer; and come together again, that Satan tempt you not for your incontinency." (1 Cor. 7:5).

Sexual intimacy can attain perfection when all the following notes of the love keyboard are played skillfully:

- *The friendly touch:* This is by far the most important touch, because friendship makes each spouse genuinely interested in the other. It helps build trust and confidence, seal their bond, reduce the sting of loneliness, wins hearts, make faults easy to correct and transform the spouses without hurting their egos.[42] It also helps them tear down the walls that separate them and create good chemistry in their relationship. Spouses who are also friends help each other shake off the hurts and the emotional wounds of the past which are a stumbling block to their mutual growth.

[42] Carnegie, Dale*: How to Win Friends and Influence People*, revised edition, (Pocket Books, 1981), pp. xxi—xxv.

They enjoy being together, staying together, working together, having fun together, and suffering together, whatever the case may be. Each spouse understands the intimate, emotional and spiritual side of the other, without judging or moralizing.

- *The pragmatic touch:* Far from being daydreamers, married people should commit to keep their feet firmly grounded, in taking realistic and practical decisions to protect their marriage and their family. When they are faced with a specific problem, they choose the most appropriate and sustainable solution. They develop a road map that shows where they are and where they are heading to. Mutual edification is enhanced in the process.
- *The passionate touch:* It is the case, for example, when a man loves his wife passionately, unconditionally, sacrificially, even if she does not deserve it. "No one never hates his own body" (Eph. 5:28–29). She plays a special role in his life, because she is the only person in the world who makes one flesh with him. On the other hand, the wife respects her husband. She matches his heart and passions with her own, by overlooking his shortfalls and seeing the very best in him (Elizabeth Bourgeret). In order

to keep their passion flame alive, the spouses celebrate each other's life and pray *with* or *for* each other regularly. Their bond is unbreakable and their love is stronger than financial hardship, illness, failures, rejection by others, or other external factors.

- *The romantic touch:* It refers to everything that promotes the couple's closeness and strengthens their relationship: compliments, good personal hygiene, sharing domestic chores, friendly pats on the back, eye contacts, hugs and other love signs which may vary from one culture to another. Romance touch is the expressive and pleasurable feeling from an emotional attraction towards another person often associated with sexual attraction.

All the love signs that a husband and a wife can use reassure the latter that she is not simply an object of pleasure, but a valued and valuable person. They also reassure her that her needs for security, understanding and compassion are taken seriously. Women connect better with people who accept them as they are. They usually want more emotional connections, while men believe that sex will create the necessary connections. When spouses find harmony in this area, when they are on the same wavelength, their bedroom becomes a haven of peace, an intimate retreat in a state of permanent blessing. It becomes, in some way, like the Holy of Holies, that sacred part of the Temple of Jerusalem to which the High Priest alone had the right of access to undertake annual rituals.

3. How to Deal with Communication Issues

Many husbands and wives feel more comfortable talking about external events, breaking news at the national or international level, or whatever is happening in their neighborhood. However, they feel less comfortable talking about their own life, their intimacy, their differences, their feelings, their emotions, their disappointments, their setbacks, their dreams, their expectations, their fears, and their hope. That is why some married people spend many years or even decades together, without really knowing one another.

To break this vicious circle, spouses should, in addition to sharing what they have heard, read, or seen in the course of the day, talk about themselves, how to build a stronger relationship, how to raise their kids, and so on. An open conversation between the spouses, leavened with a touch of humor, helps them enjoy and know each other better, resolve their conflicts peacefully and grow together (Eph. 4:29).

4. How to Deal with Spiritual Disharmony

Spiritual harmony is a difficult objective to attain, not only in a couple where one spouse is a believer and the other is not, but also when one of them is going through a spiritual transformation, while the other is not yet part of that process. Spiritual harmony is not guaranteed even when both spouses attend the same church, as their interpretation of the Word of God may differ.

It was to avoid spiritual disharmony and incompatibility in marriage that God said, "Be ye not unequally yoked together with unbelievers: for what fellowship hath righteousness with unrighteousness? and what communion hath light with darkness? And what concord hath Christ with Belial? Or what part hath he that believeth with an infidel? (2 Cor. 6:14–15)".

What can be done when a spiritual gap exists between a husband and a wife? The believing spouse should pray for the other and try to win him or her over, not only by talking the talk, but also by walking the walk, by giving a good example. Deeds speak louder than words (1 Pet. 3:1–2).

The following verses provide clear guidelines on how to handle spiritual disharmony:

> "But to the rest speak I, not the Lord: If any brother hath a wife that believeth not, and she be pleased to dwell with him, let him not put her away. And the woman which hath an husband that believeth not, and if he be pleased to dwell with her, let her not leave him. For the unbelieving husband is sanctified by the wife, and the unbelieving wife is sanctified by the husband: else were your children unclean; but now are they holy. But if the unbelieving depart, let him depart. A brother or a sister is not under bondage in such cases: but God hath called us to peace. For what knowest thou, O wife, whether thou shalt save thy husband? or how knowest thou, O man, whether thou shalt save thy wife?" (1 Cor. 7:12–16)

5. How to Deal with Child-Raising Issues

Welcomed into the world like little princes and princesses, children waste no time in making themselves the center of their parents' attention, leaving parents with little time for each other.

Children often succeed in dividing their parents by exploiting their contradictions. It happens when couples attach more importance to their parental role than to their conjugal role.

To better handle the situation, parents should give their children a good moral and spiritual upbringing, always presenting themselves with a united front. By so doing, they will help their children be better prepared for their future marriage.

The children should not be blamed for what is going on in their home, but the parents who do not discipline them or teach them what a good marriage should look like. The empty nest syndrome, which starts when grown-up children leave home, makes things worse for the spouses who have not learned how to live for each other. Some of them adjust and adapt to the realities of emptiness, but many others feel it might be too late to correct decades-long habits, and breaking up becomes an option.

6. How to Deal with In-Laws

In order to understand the environment in which each spouse grew up, each of them should, like a soil scientist who studies the soils in which plants grow, take time to learn about their respective in-laws. As part of the extended family, in-laws have a very important role to play in preparing their children for their future responsibilities as husband or wife, and eventually as father or mother. They can also be of great help when the young couple is going through a relationship crisis.

Some in-laws are a true source of support because they act like allies. When they are called upon to provide some advice on a dispute involving their son or daughter, they focus on the problem to be solved, without taking sides with their son or daughter. But other in-laws are unfair broker-dealers, as they take sides and focus on singling out the guilty spouse and apportioning all the blame to him. The obvious person they blame is naturally their son-in-law or daughter-in-law.

The most recurrent issues are those between mother-in-law and daughter-in-law. It is by no means an easy thing for a man to settle a dispute between his mother and his wife, the two people on Earth who are dearest to him. Nor is it a simple thing for two women to share the same man who is both a son and a husband. The mother-in-law can help defuse the situation by keeping her distance and only intervening when asked to do so. As for the daughter-in-law, she should treat her mother-in-law with courtesy and respect, because she is her mother too. The exemplary way in which Ruth treated her mother-in-law, Naomi, should be taken as a model by all daughters-in-law (Ruth 1:15–17).

Married persons who live far away from their families, as it is the case for Africans in the Diaspora, lack family support. So, when disputes arise between the spouses, the only option they have is to seek assistance from their friends and acquaintances. They may turn to marriage counselors or lawyers who, in spite of their good will, generally have no clue about family dynamics in other cultures.

7. How to Deal with Domestic Violence

Domestic violence usually happens when spouses have conflicting priorities or opinions. It can be verbal (belittling, yelling, screaming, intimidating, mocking, threatening, putting down, or being hostile to one another). It can become physical (grabbing, shoving, or any other means of physical assault) if both spouses get angry at the same time. Violence can be either a spur of the moment or a repeated action or habit. It is usually a sign that one spouse wants to dominate or manipulate the other. It can also be the emergence of past professional, financial, emotional or relational frustrations. Because of its serious consequences, domestic violence should be avoided at all costs. Anger management training usually helps alleviate the situation. The Scriptures teach that "The discretion of a man deferreth his anger; and it is his glory to pass over a transgression." (Prov. 19:11)[43]. Exertion of self-control requires that spouses:

- Be aware of what their partner likes and does not like, in order to avoid pushing on the wrong button. Putting oneself at the place of the other and taking into consideration how he and she would perceive what is going on and avoid aggressive arguments. To be constructive, the discussion between the spouses should be private and solution-oriented.
- Respect the rights of the other—freedom of expression, the right to be different, the right to make mistakes and learn from them, the right to enjoy emotional security, the right to love and be loved. These fundamental and alienable rights, if not taken seriously, usually trigger resentment and uncontrolled reactions.

[43] Read also Proverbs 14:29; 16:32.

- Never bring up mistakes of the past because reviving a fire which was believed extinguished often escalates the conflict.
- Never be angry at the same time. It takes two to tangle. Consequently, spouses should know how to express conflicting views, without blowing their top, without yelling at each other. They should use language and words that are not unduly offensive or disrespectful, because what is said and the way it is said can have a positive or negative impact. If a spouse absolutely wants to win an argument, the other should not fight back, because saving their relationship is far more important than winning an argument.

By so doing, the spouses will seal their relation and strengthen their faith,. An ounce of prevention is always worth a pound of cure.

Violence which cannot be controlled, or which has its roots in alcoholism or other pathological disorders, calls for a specialized assistance. A behavioral change in this case is a long and slow process, but one must never give up.

* * *

*

My spouse and I have a joint bank account, but we are not managing it properly. It happens sometimes that checks bounce, as each of us makes deposits and withdrawals without informing the other. How can we clean up this mess?

A joint bank account is a good option, as it shows that both spouses really want to lay all their cards on the table. They should, for example, determine up to what amount each of them could withdraw with a single signature, and what amount will require a double signature.

Other couples use separate accounts in order to protect themselves, for example, against the risk of losing all their hard-earned money should one of them be subject to legal proceedings, which could lead to the garnishment of their joint account.

Some couples also use a system that allows one of them to cover running costs, while the other takes care of the investment portfolio. They separate the money and split the bills—or one of them pays the bills, while the other balances the checkbook.

Others use quotas for individual participation in each budget expense category, taking into consideration their different income levels. For instance, if the husband's contribution is 60 percent for each budget item, the wife's will be 40 percent. Accordingly, if the monthly rent is $3,000 per month, the husband would pay $1,800, and the wife $1,200. If the utility bill is $250, the husband would pay $150, and the wife $100, etc.

Many other couples use a system that combines both individual and joint accounts.

There is really no standard way of managing, budgeting, saving and investing money. It is the couples' call. They should come up with a flexible system that suits them best.

Each time we manage to save some money, an expected event occurs and snatches it away. For example, a car or household appliances breaks down, an illness, a funeral, etc. How can we cope with these emergencies?

It is difficult to handle the situation with limited income, little savings, or when there is no a solid budget item for contingencies. It is already a good thing to cover such occurrences with available savings, because without those savings, getting into debt would be inevitable.

What would happen if, the wife's income is more substantial than her husband's?

The fact that a woman is in a stronger financial position than her husband usually disrupts family dynamics and trigger conflicts, because any man is expected to be the main provider in his family. Nowadays however, women have improved their level of education. It is not surprising that some of them have jobs which command good salaries. It is, indeed, a blessing for the couple, something both spouses should be happy about. When a football striker scores a goal, The victory is not his, but the team's. The same goes with marriage. Moreover, whenever the income of either spouse increases or decreases, necessary adjustments should follow. These adjustments should be income-driven, not gender-driven. This may not be a popular option, especially in sub-Saharan Africa, where a man is really a man if he is able to bear the financial burden of his family, or if he can do so with minimal assistance. Times and circumstances have changed, mentalities must change too.

There are a lot of issues and challenges in marriage. Sometimes, I just want to call it quits. What do you say about that?

My advice is DO NOT QUIT! Only quitters end up being losers. So, instead of finding reasons why you should quit, rather find reasons why you shouldn't. Fail your way to success, and do it with enthusiasm. Suffering could sometimes be the ingredient you need to move to the next level.

By the way, when I was preparing to come to the seminar, my granddaughter gave me an article[44]. Its title is "Smooth seas do not make skillful sailors." I enjoyed reading it. I learned from it, and I would like to share it with you:

> "We must experience obstacles to achieve goals. Obstacles help us build and learn the skills we need to succeed. We have to be strong in order to move through whatever we want to get through. Even when the water is calm, and there is no sign of danger, it doesn't mean you are able to control a boat. Things may end up a little harder than we expect, and we push through tough waters for things that

44 http://yogapeach.com/2012/08/14/smooth-seas-do-not-make-skillful-sailors-african-proverb/#.VsXLV7nSlDU

are worth it. If everything were easy, seamless and consistent, we wouldn't be appreciative and grateful for the good things and people in our lives. Sometimes, a storm hits to open our eyes and let go off things that no longer serve us, and see the good things we weren't paying attention to before. Smooth seas don't make skillful sailors, because the sailors don't know how to control the boat, when the sea gets rough. But when the storm comes out of nowhere and the sailor is able to manage and move forward, that's what makes a skillful sailor. Success does not happen by taking the easy route." And knowing that the challenges we face are just bumps on the road, develops endurance, courage and faith. If the cap fits, just wear it.

BISSIP: Thank you, Patriarch Bisohoñ. You said it all and we got the message in a very powerful way. All I can add is that marriage usually doesn't go away because of a huge blow-up, but because of the small leaks that accumulate over time, if forgiveness does not seal up the leaking spots. That said, let's call it a day. We will kick off tomorrow morning with Mrs. Babém's presentation.

CHAPTER 7

Don't Take Aim at the Wrong Target

Mrs. BABÉM *(The next morning):* Fables are usually the best way to get the message across. So, allow me to use the tale of *Hare, Elephant, and Hippopotamus* by Lafontaine, to drive the point home. One day, the hare wanted to find out which animal—the elephant or the hippopotamus—was the strongest one in the jungle. So, he bought a long rope and gave one end to the elephant and, some distance away, the other end to the hippopotamus. He told each of them that the other end of the rope was tied to a huge present he was offering. They were both strong, big, and powerful. Back and forth they dragged the rope, with all their might, in order to win the prize. None of them knew what was happening at the other end of the rope. The strength of each cancelled out the other. Finally, they decided to drop the tug-of-war rope to go see what was going on at the other end. They then realized how the hare had tricked them, and they declared him *persona non grata* in the jungle.

Just like the elephant and the hippopotamus, spouses must identify and neutralize the "hare" which sets them one against the other, making them fight sometimes with no valid reason. That hare is our ego, that is, our entire personality, the sum of all the disputes, disappointments, traumas and unfairness which each of us has gone through in childhood and which prevent us from full enjoyment of our marriage. Our ego is proud, illogical, and egocentric, and believes it is the standard by which everything should be measured, the center of the universe. Our ego harnesses the superiority complex, making us claim that our opinion is always better than that of our peers, and that we are more important than others. As a consequence, we cannot bear any kind of criticism, no matter how positive and constructive it may be. Our ego considers others as an obstacle or even an existential threat. Our ego is unfair and unfaithful, as it makes us believe that the person we did not marry is better than the one we married. Our ego is materialistic and individualistic; it encourages us to swear allegiance to our professional career and our self-fulfillment agenda, while sidelining our family and conjugal responsibilities.

I would like to take this opportunity to tell you a little bit about my personal experience. Being orphaned very early in life, I was raised by my grandmother. She was very indulgent and allowed me to do more or less as I liked. My wishes and desires were my boss. Whatever the size or nature of the challenges I was faced with, I handled them in my own way. I had no other authority besides myself. Any man who challenged me reaped what he sowed. I set up my "kingdom "to which only the persons who thought or behaved like me were admitted. Only in my professional life was I subject to any form of regulation, because I needed it for my survival and growth.

It is this independent woman that my husband made the mistake to marry. Once in a while, our relationship triggered a perfect storm; I perceived everything he was telling me as controlling and dictatorial, or as interference, an intrusion or an attempt to restrict my freedom. Misunderstandings and tautness that made none of us look good usually made part of our day. We managed somehow to keep together, even though we were growing apart. This sort of marriage, which is very common today, is actually a local divorce, a prelude to a spatial and legal divorce. We were almost there at least a couple of times.

There is a season for everything. My life miraculously made an unexpected U-Turn when a counselor convinced me that my resentment against my husband was actually a transference reaction, a redirection of past frustrations to my husband—the outgrowth of my "untamed and unpruned ego," so to speak. Of course, my husband was not blameless, because he would often stir things up. But is the person who shakes a bottle containing dirty water responsible for the dirt that rises up to the surface?

Happiness in marriage is not an instant gratification, but rather a crowning of the efforts of *both* spouses who are committed to work together and bring out the best in each of them. They use their differences to build a strong alliance.

My attitude towards my husband improved over the years and we have just recently celebrated our silver wedding. We are enjoying our marriage more than ever before. Yesterday, we liked being together once in a while. But today, one of us can't imagine being without the other. Yesterday, we were married but today we have a true marriage.

***

*

Does God plan and direct all marriage projects?

God is omniscient. He knows the flaws in our character and personality. He also knows the type of spouse who could help us overcome our weaknesses and live a more balanced life. But He is not going to pick that spouse. Because He gave us a certain margin for maneuvering which allows us, among other things, to choose our spouse. However, God commands that once we make a choice we should stick to it for the rest of our life.

How should we react when strongly criticized by our spouse?

Be humble and willing to learn something from it. A football player, for instance, expects to be jostled and tackled by his opponents on the field. That's how he learns not only learns how to deal with adversity, but also how to develop and sharpen his skills. The same goes for marriage. Disagreements and differences of opinions can also have a silver lining. Even if the criticism is offensive, there are some truths in it that should be taken into account.

The best way to react when criticized by our spouse is to say something like, "Honey, I cannot agree more with what you just said. If I were in your place, I would have probably said the same thing." Any escalation of the conflict could be mastered with such a courteous and positive response.

Men and women are opting more and more for free unions, because marriage has lost its appeal. Could you talk about that?

Modern women are very jealous of their independence, and they consider that marriage is taking some of it away from them. More and more women are falling in love with free unions, because they allow women to be in control, to make their own choices. A free union, however, is like candy. It has a sweet taste, but no nutritional value, and it can lead to dental decay or even diabetes in the long run. The same goes for temporary pleasures which are derived from free unions—they call for no commitment from both partners; they provide no permanence for that relation, and no security for the children which may be born; and the risk of contracting and transmitting STDs is higher with free unions than with marriages. So, why in the world would someone choose to gamble with his life in embarking on such a risky adventure?

BISSIP: Thank you, Mrs. Babém, for your faithful testimony. It appears, though, that longing after independence seems to work contrary to the principle of becoming *one flesh*. Finding a fair balance between the two is one of the main challenges couples face today. That said, let's now listen to the next speaker who will drive the nail in by stressing that no situation, no matter how critical, is hopeless. Mrs. Nwinlam, the floor is yours.

CHAPTER 8

It's Never Too Late

Mrs. NWINLAM: Laws are intended to protect us and not to harm us. That is what is taught in the following story. Ndap Lipénd, an office worker by profession, and his dog, Tutu, were inseparable friends. Tutu was aggressive and his barking scared everyone away from his territory. But his excessive aggression created a lot of problems for his master, as many complaints and even death threats were laid against his dog.

To ensure Tutu's safety, Ndap Lipénd installed an invisible electronic pet containment system, burying the wire in the ground to demarcate the area to be protected. If Tutu approached the limit of the marked territory, the electric collar he wore around his neck would give out an audible signal warning him not to go further. If he crossed the line, he would receive a mild electric shock. This happened once and he had to spend the night out, because he did not want to go through that painful experience by going back in. His master found him the next day and brought him in.

A few days later, on coming home from work, Ndap Lipénd found his dog stretched out on the grass, outside the fence. His tail did not wag as his master approached. His ears were rigid, his rear back leg was broken and his nose was bleeding. He was not breathing. Tutu was dead. He must have left the enclosure again so as to pursue intruders who may have taken their revenge against him. Ndap Lipénd broke down in tears. It was too late to remind Tutu that the invisible enclosure was not intended to restrict his liberty, but rather to protect him.

This story introduces my testimony. At a time when my husband and I were not getting on well together, one of my coworkers tried to cheer me up each day. My husband was better than this man in many respects. But there was one thing that my coworker was doing better than him—communication. I needed someone with whom I could share my troubles. My coworker provided a listening ear. He really understood me, all the more because he was going through similar problems with his own wife. Every day, we would spend a good part of our time talking about our marital problems. We were together in the office, in restaurants, the library, pretty much everywhere. Often we would keep in touch after work, by text. This permanent contact allowed him to know me better than my husband did. Gradually and smoothly, he got integrated into my life. Sometimes I would compare him to my husband and even wished that my husband could be more like him.

But instead of taking a step backwards when the idea of having an affair with him arose, I thought I was strong enough to resist that temptation. This was a big mistake because in the end I succumbed. Our friendship, which was a sinless one at the beginning, turned into an illicit and sinful relationship that went on unnoticed for two long years. During that thrilling time, I made my husband's life very miserable. I was disrespectful towards him. My uncontrolled rages ravaged our daily lives. After work, when he wanted to chat with me, I told him I was tired and he should let me sleep. When he wanted to talk to me in the morning, I told him that I was still sleeping, even though it was usually not the case. Sometimes, unusual aggressiveness in a spouse can be a sign that he is tormented by his own infidelity.

I could have continued keeping my affair secret, but since my coworker was becoming ever more demanding and possessive, I decided to cut the Gordian knot. And since I really wanted to be freed from that hypocrisy, I asked my pastor to speak to my husband about it. Feeling humiliated and betrayed, my husband made a radical decision—divorce.

I did not die physically like Tutu, but like him, my irrational behavior had serious consequences. I went through a period of moral and spiritual torment. Adapting to my new role as a divorcee with a child was a challenging task. I was tortured by regrets. I suffered stress, nightmares, headaches, stomach pains and discomfort of every kind. My blood pressure went up. I had no appetite. I felt that not only my husband, but the whole world had rejected me. My friends avoided me, because they didn't want to be contaminated by the divorce virus. They no longer invited me to their birthday parties. They no longer called me. They would not answer my phone calls. Even worse, the reception desks at the hospitals, the airports, and other public places treated couples with more courtesy than a single mom. Loneliness was my only ally.

To anesthetize my feelings of insecurity, I would go on shopping sprees. I felt so much better every time I bought a new dress, a new pair of shoes, a new handbag, or an item of jewelry. I felt I became myself again, to some extent, when I tried out a new style at the hairdresser to give myself a new look. I felt a lot better when my request to be transferred to another location was approved. This move gave me the opportunity to start a totally new life, with new friends in a new environment. It gave me the opportunity to be grounded again, to take stock of myself and find out who I truly was. To really know who you are, You need to do some soul searching. You should, as Oprah Winfrey put it, "look at yourself and accept yourself for who you are, and once you accept yourself for who you are you become a better person." I went through that uncompromising self-examination and self-analysis process.

Six years after the divorce, I met my ex-husband at the funeral of one of our former friends. And, like the fluttering eyelids of a corpse coming back to life, our love began to reawaken. We have just celebrated the seventeenth anniversary of our remarriage.

The laws in general and marriage laws in particular, are like an invisible fence that protects us from the temptations of this world. Anyone can make a mistake once, but not twice. I am now a better person, since I understand the office environment better. Professionally, I work with everyone, but I no longer take any part in the groups that form around me. I stay focused on my job. I do no longer look for close friendship at my work place, nor for emotional support from a coworker or a supervisor. My professional career is helping me to support my family and to keep it united, instead of tearing it apart because of a triangular love. My marriage is my first profession. After work, I go home, because I don't want to get involved in any wrong romance again. My husband has become the most important person in my life. I no longer do anything without consulting him first. I don't go out socially without him. I am now in my marriage and my marriage is in me.

* * *

*

What would you say are the main causes of infidelity and how can it be prevented?

The most popular causes of infidelity are the following:

- The love for money which exposes to all kinds of temptations.
- The way we were raised (old habits). People who were involved in sexual immorality as from their teen age years are usually programmed to be unfaithful partners.

Marriage does not change people; it just reveals who they really are.

- Poor connections between the spouses. This leaves too much room for a triangular love.
- Unmet physical, financial, emotional, or spiritual needs. This also enhances the risk of cheating or being cheated on, as nobody can fill the bottomless pit that needs represent.
- An overly-close friendship with a person of the opposite sex (classmates, co-workers, neighbors, etc.). Dipping into emotional issues with such people is already crossing the line. Strong boundaries must be set.
- Prolonged abstinence due to the unavailability of a spouse (long or frequent travels, illness, pregnancy and childbirth, unresolved conflicts, etc.).
- The love for sin. It is by far the major cause of infidelity. Because we plan to sin, we allow it, we endorse it, we encourage it, and we enjoy it, saying to ourselves "After all, everybody does that."

Infidelity is a choice, except in the case of a rape. Its consequences are very painful. Many people have lost their jobs, their spouses, their reputation, their wealth, their health, their lives, and even their relationship with God (Heb. 13:4), because of this addictive behavior. But is what they get better than what they lose?

Infidelity cannot be eradicated, but it can be restrained:

- If the spouses honor and value their marriage. Experience shows that the spouses who spend more time together are less exposed to temptations.
- If they treat each other as the most important person of their life.
- If they avoid socializing or traveling for pleasure without the other, unless due to serious reasons.
- If they join their forces to fight against sin; if each of them is for the other a shield against temptations.
- If they flee sexual immorality by keeping away from all sources of temptation and anything that can arouse or excite their senses such as close friendships with people of the opposite sex, erotic movies and magazines, pornographic websites, immoral audio and video clips, and the like.
- If they read the Holy Scriptures on a regular basis, so as to be forewarned and well-armed against temptations.

- If they consider the consequences that infidelity will have for themselves, their spouses, their children, their career, their health, their finances, their reputation, and their relationship with their neighbors, as well as with God.
- If they seek competent counseling when they cannot cope with a specific situation.

Loyalty is the name of game.

Should we confess our infidelity to our spouse?

Confessing infidelity is a risky business, because it is a double-edged sword. But not confessing it could be worse, especially if your spouse learns about it through other sources. Prevention is better than cure.

Can we remarry an ex-spouse?

Biblically speaking, remarriage, in general, is not acceptable as long as the ex-spouse lives. It is adultery (Rom. 7:2–3). Only a widower or a widow can remarry (1 Cor. 7:39). Remarrying an ex-spouse is only possible if, after the divorce, both spouses stayed unmarried. But if one of them married someone else in the meantime, then broke up again or became a widow or a widower, going back to the former spouse would be an abomination (Deut. 24:2–4).

God wants each marriage to be healed. It is, therefore, of the utmost importance to save the first marriage. It is by far the best one because the divorce rates for the first marriage are the lowest. In fact, nothing could provide as much joy as the first wedding dress, the first honeymoon, the first baby, the magic moments passed together as first-time spouses. Above all else, there are the blessings endowed on those who bow to divine law in staying married against all odds.

What should we do if, having remarried, we discover after the fact that we are in an adulterous relationship?

If you make one mistake by divorcing (Mal. 2:16), and a second one by remarrying (Mark 10:11–12), it would be wiser to avoid making a third mistake by divorcing again, and eventually a fourth one in remarrying again. Making a series of mistakes does not make it right. No marriage is perfect, but every marriage is worthy of respect. So we must value and protect the one we have. A bird in the hand is worth two in the bush.

When a married person has turned his back on his or her marriage and his or her spouse is tired of waiting for a reconciliation, at what point can he or she say "enough is enough" and turn that sad page?

The answers to the following questions would help determine which way to go:

- Am I blameless in the conflict I have with my spouse?
- Does God condone my decision to divorce?
- Do I also want God to forgive me for my mistakes?
- Will God forgive me, if I don't forgive my spouse?
- What impact would a divorce have on my personal life, my children, my career, or my relationship with others and with God?
- Is reconciliation still possible? If yes, at what cost?

An objective analysis of these questions will normally freeze the divorce appeal. But if after making all necessary steps that could lead to a reconciliation (Matt. 18:15–17), you realize that your spouse still wants a divorce, it must be consented to, and the separation should be a peaceful one (1 Cor. 7:15).

Experience shows that separation is usually the choice of the spouse who wants to be or is already in love with someone else. He wants to be free in order to invest more time in that new relationship.

Experience also shows that, if you don't run after someone who has abandoned you, he could one day make a U-Turn. Because love is like sea waves, it can be high or it can be low. It can go away, but it may also come back. It is not unusual that two ex-spouses get back together, especially if both of them have remained single. It takes two to tangle, and it also takes two to save a marriage. One spouse, however, could do the groundwork by making little adjustments in his behavior. However, looking desperate or begging for a reconciliation may drive the other spouse further away, as he would likely think that without him the other spouse could not survive.

The reality is that a person with a heart of flesh suffers more from a failed marriage than the person with a heart of stone. The latter usually does not see any problem divorcing and remarrying.

How should we handle a divorce?

Divorce is a bit like bereavement. To find some sanity in the midst of this chaos, you could do the following:

- Cry, because nobody marries in order to throw away all the years he has invested in the marriage, perhaps the most important part of your life.
- Pick up the remaining pieces after the crash—your children and siblings, your positive social connections, if any, your skills, your social connections and your achievements, so as to build up your self-confidence and take control of your life.
- Take stock of your own mistakes which may have somehow contributed to the break-up, with a view to learning from them.
- Forgive yourself as all the blame is not yours.
- Don't take responsibility for the faults committed by your spouse, but forgive him. The ability to forgive is a sign of humility and maturity, in contrast to the primitive desire for revenge and retaliation.

- Avoid sharing your emotional problems with your kids or with a person of the opposite sex—it is a highly confidential matter.
- Stay in touch with positive people whose assistance can help you go through this challenging experience.
- Request the assistance of trusted counselors, that is, those who can provide godly-inspired advice.
- If possible, attend a recovery seminar on subject matter.
- Read edifying books, especially the Holy Scriptures, which provide precious instructions on how to build a successful relationship.
- Help your children, if any, to adapt to the new family situation (change their leisure activities, diversify their contacts with other children of the same age group, etc.).
- Set aside some time for relaxation, but you shouldn't allow yourself to be idle when you are meant to be working.
- Take care of your physical health through a sport of your choice.
- Major on the things you can change, and don't worry about the rest. For example, it isn't your fault if your spouse does not want to change. The only person you can change is you.

- Allow time to heal your psychological wounds at a natural pace (1–3 years in some cases).

Coping judiciously with this difficult time will very probably enable you to become stronger and better equipped to help others who may face similar challenges (James 5:20).

How can a woman have the emotional security that she so desperately needs?

It is common for women today to go through painful physical and emotional experiences before marriage. Even though these are usually not spoken of, the reality is that they continue to haunt women. A woman will likely share her life experiences with her husband if she is assured that, unlike the selfish people she has known before, he has reliable emotional intelligence. She will feel more comfortable if her husband behaves, not like the Levi, but rather like the Good Samaritan (Luke 10:32–35), by doing everything it takes to heal her emotional wounds and give her hope that her future will be more glorious than her past. However, the reality is that no spouse can satisfy the needs of the other. Only God can.

BISSIP: Mrs. Nwinlam, thank you for your positive contribution. You have broken a taboo in dealing with this topic which is destabilizing many households today. The take away here is that we should never gamble with our marriage. We should take a totally different approach if we find that our current approach is not working. The next speaker will tell us how to periodically assess the status of our marriage and take corrective actions. And now, without further ado, let's invite Mr. Likenge on the podium.

CHAPTER 9

The Marriage Quiz: Am I Not the Missing Link?

LIKENGE: The quiz you are going to take is like looking at a mirror to see who you really are. It is not just having a quick glance like most men do when they are in front of a mirror, but rather like a woman who uses mirrors wherever she is to scrutinize and adjust her look.

The purpose of the fifty questions that are included in this quiz is to help you be aware of your shortcomings[45] with a view to make necessary behavioral adjustments. Your honesty will determine the quality of the results:

---

45 Family Life and Human Sexuality (FLHS) Relationship Brochure, Family Life Today (the author's name and the date don't show on this pamphlet which has been redesigned and modified by Marcel Ngué).

1. Are you aware that helping your spouse to feel less lonely and to serve him/her is your first profession?
   Yes ___ No ___
2. Do you consider your spouse as the most important person in your life (Phil. 2:3)? Yes ___ No ___
3. Do you know that strengthening your marital relationship should prevail over the accumulation of material possessions? Yes ___ No ___
4. Are you using your marriage to satisfy your personal interests at the expense of those of your spouse?
   Yes ___ No ___
5. Do you know that you belong to your spouse, not to yourself, and that your spouse should be integrated into your life? Yes ___ No ___
6. Do you often ask your spouse, "What can I do for you," instead of asking yourself what he/she is doing for you?
   Yes ___ No ___
7. Do you regularly express your appreciation of the progress your spouse is making, no matter how small, to become a better husband/wife? Yes ___ No ___

8. Do you create ideal conditions to allow your spouse to better assume his/her family and professional responsibilities? Yes ___ No ___
9. Do you think your spouse is a better person today than when you just wed? Yes ___ No ___
10. Do you respect your spouse, even though he/she might not deserve it? Yes ___ No ___
11. Are you enhancing your spouse's image by focusing on his/her qualities (Prov. 17:9), and not on his/her shortcomings? Yes ___ No ___
12. Do you stay in touch with your spouse by phone or text messages several times a day when you are not together? Yes___ No___
13. If you come home late, do you call your spouse to explain the reason for your tardiness? Yes___ No ___
14. When you get together in the evening, do you dedicate a few minutes to your spouse before getting on with your other activities? Yes ___ No ___
15. Do you take care of your household chores together? Yes ___ No ___
16. Do you cheer up your spouse when he/she is feeling depressed? Yes___ No___

17. When you have a problem, is your spouse the first person you share it with? Yes ___ No ___
18. Do you spend so much time with your cellphone, Facebook, or other social media that it eats into the time you ought to spend with your spouse? Yes___ No___
19. Do you often talk to your spouse about your sex life? Yes ___ No ___
20. Do you use sex as a tool to manipulate or punish him/her? Yes___ No___
21. Do you have a relationship, unknown to your spouse, with someone of the opposite sex who you knew before you were married? Yes___ No___
22. If a person of the opposite sex, a coworker or a friend, invites you to a party or offers you a present, do you tell your spouse about it ? Yes ___ No ___
23. Do you feel comfortable talking about your private life to a third party? Yes ___ No ___
24. Do you receive texts or phone calls that you don't want to answer, because your spouse is around? Yes___ No___
25. Do you feel more comfortable when your spouse is not around? Yes___ No___

26. When you are told to do something which negatively affects your relationship with your spouse, do you apply it? Yes ___ No ___
27. Do you and your spouse take joint decisions concerning your family budget? Yes ___ No ___
28. Do you make plans for hobbies and vacations together? Yes___ No___
29. Do you go alone to family events such as weddings, christenings, funerals, or other get-togethers, leaving your spouse at home? Yes ___ No ___
30. Do you have any personal possessions, bought since you were married, that your spouse does not know about? Yes ___ No ___
31. Do you go shopping with your spouse so that you are both aware of the market prices? Yes ___ No ___
32. If your spouse doesn't do his/her share of the household duties, do you also neglect yours? Yes ___ No ___
33. Do you think that you can do without your spouse? Yes ___ No ___
34. Do you know the buttons you should not press to avoid upsetting your spouse? Yes ___ No ___

35. Do you and your spouse often both get angry at the same time? Yes___No___
36. When your spouse absolutely wants to win an argument, do you let him/her have it? Yes ___ No ___
37. Do you still bear a grudge against your spouse for a mistake he/she may have made in the past? Yes ___ No ___
38. Do you know that God will not ask you how many times your spouse offended you, but how many times you forgave him/her? Yes ___ No ___
39. When you make a mistake, do you apologize? Yes ___ No ___
40. Do you often compare your spouse to someone else's husband or wife? Yes___ No ___
41. Do you give your children a good, Christian education so that they may grow up obedient and honest? Yes ___ No ___
42. Do you feel that your marriage is at risk because you are one flesh more with your children than with your spouse? Yes ___ No ___
43. Have you ever used the word "divorce" as a way of showing your spouse that you can't take it anymore? Yes ___ No ___

44. Do you have mutual friends, in particular older and more experienced couples, who can help you overcome your challenges? Yes ___No __
45. Do you regularly read the Holy Scriptures to learn how to handle life's challenges? Yes ___ No ___
46. Do you know that you are your spouse's keeper and his/ her closest brother/sister, and that you are accountable to God for whatever happens to him/her (Gen. 4:9)? Yes ___ No ___
47. Do you regularly pray *with* or *for* your spouse? Yes___ No ___
48. Do you know that if you do not intercede for your spouse, his/her blood will be upon you (Ezek. 33:6)? Yes ___ No ___
49. If you could start your life over again, would you still marry the same person? Yes ___ No ___
50. Did you tell a lie in answering any of these questions? Yes ___ No ___

LIKENGE: Stop! You get one point for every time you answered *Yes* to the following thirty-two (32) questions: 1, 2, 3, 5, 6, 7, 8, 9, 10, 11, 12, 13, 14, 15, 16, 17, 19, 22, 27, 28, 31, 34, 36, 38,

39, 41, 44, 45, 46, 47, 48 and 49. You also score one point if you answered *No* to the eighteen (18) following questions: 4, 18, 20, 21, 23, 24, 25, 26, 29, 30, 32, 33, 35, 37, 40, 42, 43 and 50.

Your results will remain confidential. Discuss them with your spouse and take corrective measures. If you scored gold or silver (see the answer grid below), please check your answers again carefully.

Answer grid

Points	Comments
0–24	***Wood:*** The spouses in this category have almost nothing in common. Each of them thinks that the other is an obstacle to his/her progress. Their conversation is focused on the bills to be paid, nothing about their relationship. As a consequence, they can live together for years like roommates without really knowing each other. Such a *cold love* deepens the loneliness of both spouses. Those who live that way end up filing for divorce. Others continue to endure their marriage instead of enjoying it.
25–40	***Bronze:*** The spouses like talking about big events, not too much about themselves. It is a *lukewarm love* that shows that each spouse needs the other periodically. The sting of loneliness is less damaging, even though self-centeredness and self-interest are still having some good days.

41–45	***Silver:*** The spouses are aware that love is not instant gratification, but the result of hard work by spouses who want to become one flesh. It is a *developing love* that allows the spouses to exchange ideas on how to integrate their lives, in spite of daily challenges; and how to keep improving their relationship through frequent interactions with more experienced couples.
46–50	***Gold:*** The spouses frequently include intimacy in their conversations, by sharing their emotional and sexual expectations, their frustrations, their progress and their hope. They support each other and promote mutual edification. They pray *with* or *for* each other. Since a boat is never too large to capsize, they evaluate their performance on a regular basis in order to adjust their sails and keep moving in the right direction. It is a *mature, mutual, stable and selfless relationship*.

This quiz will help you shape up and start out anew, like the eagle of Somapan (Chapter 4). Use this tool to develop a progressive improvement plan, set daily goals, and remind yourselves consistently of what they are. For example, your first objective could be to never go to bed with an argument that has not been settled. The second objective could be to never bring up mistakes of the past. Set a reasonable time frame to achieve each objective (month to month). When the first objective is met, no matter how long it takes, move on to the next one, and so forth. It is a lifetime training process. Practice makes perfect. Becoming the main agent of change in your household should be your ultimate goal. Good luck!

BISSIP: Thank you, Mr. Likenge, for this excellent tool. I would invite you to share it with your friends and your neighbors. Although we covered a lot of ground in two days, more still needs to be done. As you may have noticed, we focused on connections and relationship-building more than on family budget and financial management issues—hence the title of the seminar: *Relationship Development and the Family.* The reality is that people like to do business with people they get along with. That is why, when spouses know each other and accept each other, everything else falls into place. In this case, even discussions about money will likely be less stressful. That said, let's now give our undivided attention to Patriarch Bisohoñ for the closing remarks.

BISOHOÑ: Ladies and gentlemen, brevity is the soul of wit. The best speech is usually a short one. Mine should have been as short as the distance between the rooster's eye and his beak. But I would like to take this opportunity to share an important message. One day, an elder from Tamaloñ invited a young man home to help him chop some wood. Not being offered any remuneration for this work, the young man declined the invitation. Another young man who was nearby heard the conversation and offered his services. On arriving at destination, however, he was stunned to find out that chopping wood was not in view, but rather the celebration of the old man's eightieth birthday! It isn't easy to read wise men's minds because they usually don't mean what they say. The young man in this story was me, sixty years ago. I offered my assistance, not to get any compensation, but just to serve. It is in this same spirit that you must approach your marriage. Your vow should be to give, to serve and do whatever is right for your spouse.

It is a challenge, and a very big one, to keep doing the same things over and over, with the same motivation, the same devotion and the same enthusiasm. Loyalty should always prevail. But, "Better is it that thou shouldest not vow, than that thou shouldest vow and not pay." (Eccles. 5:5; 7:5). That said, I declare the Boonjok seminar closed. May God richly bless you all.

The participants still hung around for a few minutes, taking the time to exchange names, phone numbers, and email addresses.

The seminar led to a fundamental change in the way Saba and Nléla would relate to each other. They promised to discuss how to apply the lessons learned to their current situation.

PART THREE

Inside the Chrysalis' Cocoon

CHAPTER 10

Time Out!

Like a caterpillar which has stored up reserves and closes itself up inside a cocoon to undergo its metamorphosis, Saba and Nléla took some time out to think about their contradictions and inconsistencies. Beyond the chrysalis-like state they were in, their hope was to soar above their differences in order to achieve the beauty and lightness of a butterfly. Their meditations below reflect their paradigm shift.

1. Nléla's monologue

My mind is full of mixed messages. One side of my brain is telling me, "Nléla, why would you want to be caught up again in a stressful relationship with that man who doesn't even appreciate the blessing he has to be married to a special person like you?

Don't you know that most men would give their right arm to win your heart? Close this sorry chapter and move on."

But the other side of my brain is telling me something quite different, "Nléla, the power of reconciliation is greater than that of divorce. How many new starts have you made in life so far, and have you found the happiness you were seeking? Swallow your pride and think about the well-being of your children. They want to live in a stable home under the supervision of both parents." I ought to be kinder to my husband, treating him as I'd wish him to treat me, and not doing to him what I wouldn't wish him to do to me. Instead of asking what he can give me, I should ask myself what I can do for him. I will integrate him in my life and involve him in whatever I do. Better the devil you know than the devil you don't know. But before we can get back together, he will have to prove his love by persuading me that things will no longer be the same. He won't surely be in for an easy ride, because a woman's trust, once lost, is not that easy to reconquer.

Several kilometers away, Saba too was going through self-examination.

2. *Saba's monologue:*

My marital troubles have made me realize the extent of my own vulnerability, because one can truly measure the height of a tree only when it has been brought down. I regret having dedicated more time and energy to my professional career and my friends than to my marriage. So, just as a shower of rain doesn't put off a lover's appointment, and no distance is ever too far for a lover, I will overcome any obstacle on my way to meet Nléla and tell her: "*Apple of my eye,* forgive me for extending your emotional wilderness. But wilderness can also be the way to Canaan[46]. From now on, I will do my best to truly know you, to understand your feelings and your motivations, to give you my undivided attention and to love you, because you are the most important person in my life. And to prove it, I will offer you a weekend near a beach at my expense, either at Kribi or Limbe, to discuss how to go from here. Even if you do no longer care about spending time with me, at least allow me to have some input in your healing process."

---

[46] Canaan was the name of a large and prosperous country which corresponds roughly to present-day Lebanon, Syria, Jordan and Israel and was also known as Phoenicia. Before conquering this land, the Israelites spent forty years in the wilderness. It was the consequence of their disobedience to God. Canaan symbolizes a glorious life that comes after a painful experience.

If Nléla offers me another chance, I will take it with both hands. But, if she decides otherwise, I will be disappointed, but not discouraged, because what cannot be cured must be endured. Happiness, after all, is the sum of all the problems I don't have.

* * *

As promised, Saba made the offer of a reconciliatory trip to Nléla. She turned it down, and made a counter offer instead - having a phone conversation that would help them to lay down the ground rules for their new relationship. Much has changed after five years apart and putting matters straight again is no easy task. A number of sticking points meant the negotiations became bogged down several times. Because when an agreement couldn't be reached, Nléla would bring the conversation to an abrupt halt by hanging up the phone. She wanted to show how difficult it was for her husband to gain her allegiance back. The assistance of a renowned broker-dealer helped avoid the worst.

3. Telepsép, the "Firefighter"

After listening to Saba and Nléla, Telepsép had this to say: "Love can go and love can come back, if there is true repentance and genuine forgiveness. A happy marriage is not a smooth ride, rather it is the union of two spouses who's will to forgive and reconcile is stronger than their differences. Better bend than break. Your reconciliation was closest when it looked further away. High emotions are sometimes the prelude of a more thrilling relationship. Like the contractions of a woman in labor intensify as the moment of birth approaches, the frequency of your stormy arguments is the lead-up to a new birth, certainly the birth of a happier life. Both of you have identified what you like and what you don't like, and you came up with appropriate and balanced recommendations. Doing what you promised to do is the next step. For the time being, your homework will be to write a love letter to each other. Do not hesitate to contact me, should you need further assistance."

Well aware that the outlook for his marriage was far from serene, in spite of a few gleams of sunlight, Saba decided to defer the decision to write a love letter, as he did not want to put the cart before the horse. He wanted to be his wife's friend besides being her husband. So, he began to look at his marriage as though he were an explorer, rather than just a tourist. He started courting his wife as it was the case the very first time they had a date. He thought it was better to work on his marriage than to romance another woman, as it would take the same amount of effort, if not more, to build a strong relationship. He took time to better understand the intimate, emotional and spiritual side of his wife, without judging or moralizing. His wife did the same. They left nothing to chance. They increased contacts through telephone calls, emails, texts, family gatherings and the like. Later, to achieve a closer relationship, they began meeting, usually in secluded places. During these meetings, they talked about their best souvenirs, avoiding issues that might oppose them. They laughed a great deal. They walked in the park, hand in hand, exchanging friendly pats. They ate in various restaurants. They played and danced together. They found ways to connect even in their dreams.

But once a coconut has dried up, it has to fall. So, once their small-step strategy had brought them to the right moment, they decided to follow Telepsép's advice. During a meeting behind closed doors during which each read a love poem addressed to the other; both broke down in tears. This was a necessary move towards a more harmonious life. For five years, God had been preparing for this moment. After the rains, comes the good weather!

CHAPTER 11

The Three Main Qualities of the Ideal Spouse

To avoid repeating their past mistakes, Saba and Nléla chose the three following qualities which would help them live a more fulfilling life. These three qualities are reminiscent of a tortoise:

1. Tender in the inside;
2. Tough on the outside;
3. A head sticking out of the shell to scrutinize the horizon.

1. Tender in the inside

Tenderness of heart is the first quality which they intend to nurture. Just like a tortoise, whose soft flesh is hidden inside its shell, Saba and Nléla want to have a "heart of flesh" and not a "heart of stone" (Ezek. 11:19; 36:26). They have taken inspiration from a recent story which, even if it did not deal with marriage, shows how they can better connect with and be a good medicine for the other. Two patients were sharing a room at the Sakbayeme hospital. Every afternoon, Manyodi had to sit still for an hour to have his lungs drained. Since his bed was by the window, he took the opportunity to tell Paglan, his roommate, what was going on in the nearby park. Ducks and swans were swimming in a big pond full of fish. Runners competed against each other on a track around the pond. Lovers wandered together underneath large, beautiful trees or by colorful flower beds, while children flew their kites. A little farther off, small boats were crossing the Sanaga River, helping passengers to travel from Sakbayeme to Soñ Mbenge and back. The blue skies stretched to the horizon. As if he were a journalist, Manyodi reported new events every day.

Paralyzed and lying on his back, Paglan listened, entranced, to these lively and fascinating descriptions by his roommate.

What he heard made him feel in some way still in touch with the outside world.

Then one day, tragedy stroke. Manyodi died in his sleep of a massive heart attack. Paglan mourned the passing of his friend for a very long time. Eventually, he asked, and was granted permission, to move to the bed by the window so that he could comfort himself by observing what was happening outside. He was stunned, however, when he realized that a neighboring building completely blocked the view. When a nurse came in the room, he asked her: "How could Manyodi see, from this window, all the scenes he was describing every day?" The nurse's reply was unequivocal. "Manyodi could not see anything, not only because of this building which blocks the view, but also because he was legally blind. However, since he did not want you to feel lonely, he did his very best every day to put a smile on your face, to make life seem more pleasant to you, even though his own life was anything but pleasant."

This story taught the Sabas that *empathy* and *altruism* should be among the main qualities they should identify themselves with, in order to build a permanent bridge between them. They are determined to sow good seeds in each other's heart, by using words that build up trust and confidence. They will put themselves in each other's shoes in order to create more chemistry between them.

2. Tough on the outside

To be tough on the outside is the other quality that the Sabas are determined to enhance. Just as the shell of a tortoise is a protection from bad weather and predators, the couple wants to feel sheltered from all kinds of threat. The story of the donkey miraculously saved inspired them. The donkey fell into a deep well during the dry season. Unable to get it out of the well, the farmer decided to fill in the hole, so that no child could one day find himself at the bottom of the pit. At his request, the villagers started work. The donkey bleated as the lumps of earth fell down onto his back. Then his cries died away. The old farmer thought that the animal must have died and was already buried. He was stunned when, glancing down the hole to see how much it had filled up with soil, he saw that the donkey was still alive and well grounded! As brave as Mr. Seguin's goat when faced with the wolf[47], the donkey faced the challenge with a winner's mentality, and never let the pain be stronger than his survival instinct. And

47 A tale by Alphonse Daudet. The only difference is that Mr. Seguin's goat did not survive, in spite of his courage in the face of the wolf.

as the earth showered down on him, he shook it off each time and stepped on it. By so doing, the animal succeeded in climbing further up at each move. And when the hole was almost filled up, he was able to leap out with a broken leg. His life was safe.

This is the kind of endurance and courage that the Sabas hope to develop. They are determined to build up a strong character which will enable them to face up courageously to the harsh realities of life which will surely assail them just like those clumps of earth. They will use the bricks that life is throwing at them - marital and family issues, job loss, illness, injustice, rejection, persecution, and so on - to build a stronger relationship. The more challenging the situations, the more determined they will be to face them. In the face of adversity, they will not soften like carrots in hot water, but rather toughen up like boiled eggs, or even better, like clay bricks baked in the sun.

3. A head sticking out of the shell to scrutinize the horizon

This is the third quality to which the Sabas aspire. Like the head of a tortoise sticking out of the shell to scrutinize the horizon and check if there is any imminent danger, the Sabas are determined to lift up their eyes unto the hills to seek God's assistance and protection (Ps. 21:1–2). The story about the Israelites looking upon the bronze serpent mounted by Moses on a pole in the wilderness to survive the bites of poisonous serpents' bites[48] has inspired them.

They are aware that he who has the palm nuts has palm oil. Similarly, he who has God has the solution to all his problems. This assurance motivates them to go out of their comfort zone and follow God's script in whatever they are doing.

These three basic qualities represent the solid foundation upon which the Sabas will build their relationship and raise their kids. Their first step will be the renewal of their vows.

48 The bronze serpent functioned as a cure against the bite of fiery serpents sent by God to punish rebellious people of Israel (Num. 21:6–9).

CHAPTER 12

An Unusual Renewal of Vows

Several months later, having decided on the parameters which will henceforth govern their life, Saba, accompanied by Nléla, hastened to inform their children about the good news. "My dear children," he said, "I am sorry for the wrong choices I made and that have resulted in our family being divided for so long. But the good news is that all of that is now history. In a few weeks' time, we will celebrate a special family reunion as your parents are soon going to renew their vows".

The children's faces, at first tense, gradually relaxed as they heard the breaking news. Their father's words and their mother's smile reassured them.

The clock started ticking and when D-day came, Saba and Nléla made a triumphant entry in the Village Hall, amidst the applause of their guests. When the applause finally died down, Telepsép spoke.

TELEPSÉP: Dear relatives and dear friends, please be seated. *(Turning to Mr. and Mrs. Sabasaba)* Place yourselves eight steps away from me, one of you on my left-hand side and the other on my right. I am going to ask you eight questions to which you should reply. For the sake of fairness, if one of you provides the first answer to a question, he or she will allow the other spouse to provide the first answer to the next question. There are no wrong answers, because you will just be expressing your own wishes. After each answer, you will move one step towards each other.

When everything was in place, Telepsép went through the questions:

Question # 1: Do you desire to freely renew your marriage vows?

SABA: Yes, I do.

NLÉLA: Yes, I do.

Question # 2: Do you promise to live for your spouse and not for yourself?

NLÉLA: Yes, I do.

SABA: Yes, I do.

Question # 3: What is more important for the survival of your marriage—your rights or your duties?

SABA: My duties.

NLÉLA: My duties.

Question # 4: Who is your greatest enemy?

NLÉLA: My pride.

SABA: My selfishness.

Question # 5: What is the greatest gift you can give your spouse?

SABA: Love.

TELEPSÉP: To love your wife is to want the best for her. It is to be concerned not only for her physical and material well-being, but also and above all for her eternal life.

NLÉLA: *[She is still taking time to come up with an answer. After conferring briefly with Saba, she says]:* Respect.

TELEPSÉP: Respect is indeed the greatest gift you can give to your husband. It means behaving like an ally, giving him advice when necessary, but not orders.

Question # 6: What would you do if your expectations were not met?

NLÉLA: I would continue to assume my responsibilities and trust the rest to God.

SABA: I would keep in mind that love is more about giving than about receiving.

Question # 7: What is the most important legacy you can leave to your children?

SABA: A united and happy family.

NLÉLA: The fear of God.

TELEPSÉP: Now, we have arrived at the eighth and last question. At this point, only one more step separates the two of you. You both know what to do, once you have taken that last step, don't you?

Question # 8: What nickname have you chosen for your spouse?

NLÉLA: Commitment.

SABA: Empathy.

And suddenly, like a goalkeeper diving for a ball, both spouses threw themselves on one another. Cries of happiness, ululations from the women, the flash of many cameras, accompanied this most unusual event. The uproar of the crowd only came down when Telepsép spoke. He had a message for the couple.

TELEPSÉP: I'd just like to stress that, as our tradition dictates, names are not given randomly or from a calendar listing. They have a special meaning, because they describe the quality of the hero a child should resemble. Sometimes, names can also refer to a prophecy. It is, therefore, our hope that "Commitment" and "Empathy" will become a new way of life inviting you to thrive for excellence, being loyal and faithful to one another, living for one another, for better or for worse, in wealth or in poverty, in health or in sickness, till death do you part. If you agree with what you heard, say: "Yes, I do."

SABA: Yes, I do.

NLÉLA: Yes, I do.

TELEPSÉP: You said it. Where there is a will, there is a way. May God richly bless you.

On their way out, the two spouses expressed their feelings:

NLÉLA: I am so moved that I don't know what to say:

Yesterday, I was lonely and hopeless.
Today, I am with my husband.
Let's celebrate and be merry.
For my marriage was dead, but now is alive.
I thank all those who prayed for us
While a *tsunami* was sweeping away
Our family history.

SABA: The caterpillar has now become a butterfly and is out of the cocoon. New life has begun. That is why we are celebrating the victory of humility over pride, forgiveness over retribution, selflessness over selfishness, self-denial over self-fulfillment, friendship over rivalry, compassion over indifference, commitment over carelessness. We know that any small, but crucial step in the right direction will likely trigger new challenges. But when the roots are deeply grounded, the tree is able to hold out against any storm.

The celebrations then continued as planned. The photographers were committed to immortalize every step of the celebration. The participants included, among others: Kasimanga and Kétura; Kunyakunya and Mpesa; Sipora; Deborah and Mbônji; the representatives of VILMA; the in-laws from both families; and numerous friends and acquaintances.

In the evening, the guests' attention was drawn to the children of the Saba family who, with their friends, had formed a small circle in the center of the room. They danced and danced, surrounded by adults, until the small hours of the morning. It was a party within a party.

Indeed, an unbreakable alliance between the parents is, far more than toys or clothes, the best gift that they can offer to their children.

CONCLUSION

A Marriage above the Clouds

Nowadays, marriage continues to appeal, even though it inspires more fear than ever before. To be on the safe side, many people look to those who have been there for guidance. But only those who consider marriage to be an indivisible and lifetime union between a man and a woman may truly enjoy its fruit. Although they come from different walks of life, people who are happily married have a few things in common. They give more than they receive. They know that a successful marriage is not an instant gratification, but rather a commitment to thrive for excellence. They reject current rebellious philosophies and immoral cultural trends that are waging a relentless war against marriage as ordained by God.

Such spouses have become as rare as the hair on the bald man's head. Some biblical characters are the best role models. Sarah, for example, is the perfect example of devotion incarnate.

She demonstrated an exemplary level of respect for her husband, Abraham. She obeyed him and called him her *lord* (1 Pet. 3: 6).

The same goes for Abraham who proved that his love for his wife was greater than her barrenness. She was more valuable to him than Hagar, their Egyptian maid who, after giving Abraham his first son, Ishmael, started despising her mistress. To show his unconditional love for Sarah, Abraham told her, "Behold, thy maid is in thy hand; do to her as it pleaseth thee. And when Sarai dealt hardly with her, she fled from her face." (Gen. 16:6).

It is also the case of Elkanah who, like Abraham, proved that Hannah's barrenness was not a liability. He loved her more than his other wife, Peninnah, who had children and enjoyed making fun of Hannah's barrenness. When Elkanah realized that Hannah could no longer bear the mockery of her rival, he told her, "Hannah, why weepest thou? And why eatest thou not? And why is thy heart grieved? Am not I better to thee than ten sons?" (1 Sam. 1:8).

Later on, God wiped the tears of both Sarah and Hannah by blessing their wombs and they finally had children.

Another inspiring example is that of Rebecca who, after the death of her mother-in-law Sarah, gave to her husband Isaac the moral and psychological support he needed to get through this painful experience. She was like a second mother to him (Gen. 24:67).

The attitude of Abigail, the wife of Nabal, is also very inspiring. Her husband was so wicked and so proud that he even challenged King David's authority. After failing to obey the king's orders, he had the nerve to ask, "Who is David?" (1 Sam. 25:10). When David decided to give him an exemplary punishment, Abigail took her husband's misconduct upon herself. Her humble attitude, her respectful words, and the conciliatory gift she offered to the king helped alleviate the situation. Instead of blaming her husband for his faults or betraying him, she instead chose to intercede on his behalf (1 Cor. 7:14). She acted like his defense attorney.

Another great example is that of Zechariah and Elizabeth, the parents of John the Baptist. Their mutual desire to properly serve God strengthened not only unity in their ministry, but also unity in their vision and their faith (Luke 1:6). Such a unity between husband and wife is, in the eyes of God, more valuable than material possessions and temporary pleasures.

However, the most shining example is that of the virtuous woman (Prov. 31:10–31). She accepts her responsibilities (Eph. 5:22–23) fully and not partially, joyfully and not reluctantly. It is a pleasure for her to serve. Her qualities are clearly spelled out in the following verses[49].

- She is worthy of trust (verse 11).
- She is a source of encouragement and motivation for her husband (verses 11–12).
- She is hard-working and full of energy (verses 13–17; 24 and 27).
- She is self-disciplined (verse 15).
- She is not corrupt (verse 18).
- She is generous and compassionate towards her husband (verses 19–20).
- She shows forethought (verse 21), and ability to cope with life's challenges.
- She lives for her husband and her children, and not for herself (verse 21).
- She protects and enhances her husband's image (verse 23).
- She has no fear for the future (verse 25), because she trusts in God, who protects and feeds even the animals (Matt. 6:24–26).

[49] Rev. Charles Stanley, In Touch Ministry, Atlanta, Georgia.

- She has dignity (verse 25), because she knows, not *who* she is, but *whose* she is—she belongs to God through her husband.
- She weighs her words before speaking (verse 26), and only wise and useful words come from her mouth.
- She oversees everything that happens in her household (verse 27).
- She is valued by her husband and her children (verse 28).
- She is worthy of praise because she lives in the fear of God (verse 30).
- She manifests her faith through her good works (verse 31).

The degree of devotion, humility, loyalty and commitment shown by this woman is quite out of the ordinary. Her happiness does not depend on what her husband does for her, but on what she does for him. She does not love him "as long as," "given that," "on condition that," or "only if" he meets certain criteria. Her love is unconditional and even sacrificial (Agape love).

Such qualities can only be found in a woman who is not defined by the "outward adorning of plaiting the hair, and of wearing of gold, or of putting on of apparel; But let it be the hidden man of the heart, in that which is not corruptible, even the ornament of a meek and quiet spirit, which is in the sight of God of great price." (1 Pet. 3:3–4).

It is clear, upon close examination of this woman's profile, that no person in flesh and blood could fit that bill. Only God's spirit can bring about such selfless love. That woman is an inspiration not only for other women, but also for men, for every human being, regardless of gender, color, race, or origin, who desires to move closer to Christ and become one with Him (1 Cor. 6:17). She symbolizes the perfection of the Eternal Church, the select group of people who are, or will be saved.

In spite of some disappointments, God makes no secret of His love for His earthly representatives, as evidenced by His love for the Jewish nation and for the Church.

God's love for the Jewish nation

God's relationship with the Jewish nation is not a master-slave relationship, nor even like the relationship between a king and his subjects, but rather like the union of a husband and a wife. This is what the following passage is teaching:

"For thy Maker is thine **husband**; the LORD of hosts is his name; and thy Redeemer the Holy One of Israel; The God of the whole earth shall he be called. For the LORD hath called thee as **a woman** forsaken and grieved in spirit, and a wife of youth, when thou wast refused, saith thy God." (Isa. 54:5–6).

Thus, God was very disappointed when His people, whom He had adopted and loved so dearly, whom He had miraculously brought out of Egypt, whom He had protected from powerful enemies, betrayed Him by committing spiritual adultery and becoming idolatrous, rebellious, and faithless. His disappointment is described in the following passage.

> "Surely as **a wife** treacherously departeth from **her husband**, so have ye dealt treacherously with me, O house of Israel, saith the LORD." (Jer. 3:20). Read also: verses Jer. 30:22, 31–32).

The break was therefore inevitable (Jer. 3:8, 31–32). But why did God who hates divorce (Mal. 2:16) break His alliance with the Jewish people? And does not Moses' certificate of divorce (Deut. 24:1) confirm that divorce is an option? It is true that both moves would appear to endorse divorce. But they need to be viewed in their historical context. God's rejection of the Jewish nation, for example, was a temporary measure (Rom. 11:25) reflecting His wish to quash an idolatrous, rebellious and faithless people, after their escape from Egypt.[50] Since God is not emotion-driven, but acts in accordance with His laws, He conceived the law on divorce to meet the needs of the case. But to ensure that divorce would not inspire imperfect mankind, He made a very important point.

> "And said, For this cause shall a man leave father and mother, and shall cleave to his wife: and they twain shall be one flesh? Wherefore they are no more twain, but one flesh. What therefore God hath joined together, let not man put asunder." (Matt. 19:5–6). Read also: Mark 10: 9.

God's Love for the Church

The break with the Jewish nation led God to create a new bond with the Gentiles, the non-Jews across the world, through the Holy Church, in the context of the New Testament. He took this opportunity also to point out that:

> "Behold, the days come, saith the LORD, that I will make a new covenant with the house of Israel, and with the

[50] Read also Isa. 50:1; 59:2; La. 1:5.

house of Judah: Not according to the covenant that I made with their fathers in the day that I took them by the hand to bring them out of the land of Egypt; which my covenant they brake, although **I was a husband** unto them, saith the LORD: But this shall be the covenant that I will make with the house of Israel; After those days, saith the LORD, I will put my law in their inward parts, and write it in their hearts; and will be their God, and they shall be my people." (Jer. 31:33).

Nevertheless, the alliance with the Church was also disrupted by its disobedience, right from the first generation (Apoc. 2 and 3). The seven local churches in these two chapters represent all the past, present and future local Churches. The fact that all of them were destroyed or died out constitutes a serious warning for contemporary churches[51].

The only Church in view, as from Apocalypse 4, is not a local denomination, but the Eternal Church, all the "true worshippers" of Christ (John 4:23). They are His spiritual wife (Eph. 5:25; Apoc. 21:2, 9).

---

51 Re.2:4.

There will be no physical marriage in the New World (Matt. 22:30). The role of this marriage is to teach, among other things, that each man in the image of Christ, should love his wife unconditionally, being concerned not only for her physical and material well-being, but also and above all for her eternal life; and that each woman should submit to her husband, as the spiritual Church is submitted to Christ (Eph. 5:22–24).

Hence, physical marriage is a training opportunity. It is also a crucial link in God's salvation plan, as it allows spouses to develop qualities that would accompany them into eternity. It could even be a more fulfilling experience if Christian communities join their forces to become the last bastions of defense for the family based on the union of a man and a woman with a view to procreation; and if those communities become a prophetic voice which, like that of John the Baptist in the wilderness, cries out against any doctrinal change relating to marriage and the family, and against any redefinition of god-ordained marriage.

Like a finger (the signifier), the marriage between a man and a woman is pointing towards something greater, namely Christ's eternal love for the chosen ones (the signified). Hence, like the new moon or the Sabbath, marriage is "the shadow of things to come; but the body is of Christ." (Col. 2:16–17). In other words, all those things will find their fulfillment in Christ.

However, in the light of the unfaithfulness and faithlessness shown by His earthly representatives, God is no longer interested in any alliance with a whole nation, a whole people or a whole institution. He is interested in an alliance with individuals chosen at His own discretion. That is what the following verses are teaching:

> Then shall two be in the field; the one shall be taken, and the other left. Two women shall be grinding at the mill; the one shall be taken, and the other left." (Matt. 24: 40–41).

The eternal marriage with Christ is, therefore, the only hope for all believers, men or women, married or single, with or without children, who feel physically or emotionally isolated, abused, denigrated, mocked, oppressed, humiliated, betrayed, exploited, emasculated, or rejected by those whose duty is to accept them and be compassionate towards them. They should keep assuming their responsibilities, with love and commitment, even in a hostile environment, while awaiting, like Cinderella, the glorious arrival of the Prince (Apoc. 19:9). The chosen ones will then be caught up in the clouds to meet Him in the air (1 Thess. 4:17).

Like a groom who gets his home ready to welcome the bride, Christ has gone to prepare a place in Heaven for us, so that, He said, "Where I am, there ye may be also." (John 14: 3).

Soon, we will experience the joy of eternal life with a faithful, loyal and almighty Spouse (Isa. 54:5–6), and nothing could ever "separate us from the love of God, which is in Christ Jesus our Lord." (Rom. 8:39).

Long live marriage!

Selected Bibliography

- *The Holy Bible,* New King James Version, Cambridge University Press, USA. http://www.kingjamesbibleonline.org
- *Bible,* traduction française, version Louis Second, 1910
- *Cruden's Complete Concordance to the Bible,* edited by John Eadie, Dugan Publishers, Inc., Gordonsville, TN, USA, 1986.
- *Dictionnaire biblique pour tous,* Les Éditions Ligue pour la Lecture de la Bible (L.L.B.), Valence Cedex, France, 1989.
- *The New Revised Standard Version Bible,* Division of Christian Education of the National Council of Churches of Christ in the United States of America, Copyright©1989.
- *The Student Bible Dictionary,* a complete learning system to help you understand words, people, places, and events of the Bible, Karen Dockrey, Johnnie & Phillis Godwin, Barbour Publishing, Inc. , 2000, Uhrichsville, OH, USA.

***

*

Anderson, David A. (Pastor): *I Forgrace You, Doing Good to Those Who Have Hurt You,* Intervarsity Press, Copyright©2011.

Avini Aloys: *Un amour qui meurt n'a jamais existé,* Les Presses universitaires de Yaoundé (Lespuy), 2001.

Bessala, Jacques Lagrâce: *Mariage et vie du couple aujourd'hui,* Imprimerie Saint Paul, Yaoundé, 2010.

Bafinamene Kisolokele, Charles: *La stérilité du couple: Approche théologique et pastorale en milieu ecclésial négro-africain.* Mémoire de Maîtrise en Théologie, Faculté de théologie évangélique de Bangui, RCA, septembre, 2009. https://palabre.files.wordpress.com/2009/01/sterilite_ch_k_bafinamene_1999a.pdf

Biéler, André: *L'homme et la femme dans la morale calviniste,* Collection Nouvelle série théologique, Labor & Fides, Genève, 1963.

Biton Koulibaly, Isaïe:

- *Ah! Les femmes,* Nouvelles, les classiques ivoiriens, 2è édition, Éditions Haho, 1987.
- *Ah! Les hommes,* Nouvelles, les classiques ivoiriens, Éditions Haho, 1991.
- *Encore les femmes . . . toujours les femmes,* Nouvelles, les classiques ivoiriens, Éditions Haho, 1995.

Calvin, Jean: *Commentaires sur l'Ancien Testament,* texte établi par Pierre Marcel, Labor & Fides, Genève, 1961.

Camping, Harold:

- *What God Hath Joined Together,* Family Radio Inc., Oakland, California, USA, 1997.
- *Gay Pride, un signe de la fin des temps planifié par Dieu,* Family Stations, Inc. Oakland, California, USA, 2010.

Carnegie, Dale: *How to Win Friends & Influence People,* Gallery Books, New York, USA, Copyrights 1936.

Casterman, Jean-Benoît: *Pour réussir ta vie sentimentale et sexuelle, À toi qui veux aimer et être aimé(e),* Réservé à qui cherche le Big Love. SOPECAM, Yaoundé, Cameroun, janvier 2011.

Chapman, Gary:

- *L'amour dans l'impasse, Quand l'avenir du couple semble compromis,* Farel Éditions, Cedex 2, France, 2è édition, 3è impression, 2005.
- *Things I Wished I'd Known before We Got Married,* Copyrighted material, 2005.

Clark, David E. & William G.: *Married but Lonely: Seven Steps You Can Take with or without Your Spouse's Help,* SILOAM, Charisma media/Charisma House Book Group, Florida, USA, Copyright©2013.

Dag Heward-Mills: *Le mariage modèle, un guide en matière de conseils matrimoniaux* (traduction), Lux Verbi, BM (Pty), Ltd., Wellington, South Africa, copyright©2009.

Djebba, Fidèle: *Cœur de femmes,* Nouvelles, Éditions Clé, Yaoundé, 2012.

Dobson, James: *Love Must Be Tough, New Hope for Marriages in Crisis*, Multnomah Publishers, 1983.

Eloundou, Simon: *L'Amour en Soi-même*, Éditions Clé, Yaoundé, Cameroun, 2010.

Etoundi Fouda, Hippolyte: *Conseils pratiques pour le mariage*, Éditions Bénévent, 2003.

Evans, Tony (Pastor):

- *Kingdom Man: Every Man's Destiny, Every Woman's Dream*, Tyndale House, USA, 2012.
- *For Married Men Only: Three Principles of Loving Your Wife*, Moody Publishers, USA, 2010.
- *For Married Women Only: Three Principles For Honoring Intimacy*, Moody Publishers, USA, 2010.

Foti, Jean-Pierre (Abbé): *Préparation au mariage*, Quelques grandes lignes, 3è édition revue et augmentée, Bafoussam, août 2006.

Hunt, June: *Forgiveness, the Freedom to Let Go,* Hope for the Heart, Rose Publishing/Aspire Press, Torrance, California 90503, USA, Copyright©2013.

Jean-Paul II: *Catéchisme de l'Église catholique,* Paris, Marne-Librairie, Éditrice vaticane/Plon, 1992.

Kennedy, D. James: *Save a Marriage, Save our Nation,* A guide to Domestic tranquility, Coral Ridge Ministries, Florida, USA, 2005.

Kimmel, Tim & Darcy: *Grace in the Bedroom,* from the series: Grace Filled Marriage, Family Life Today, USA, April 2014.

Kuemo, Michel: *Le mariage d'aujourd'hui, amateurisme ou professionnalisme,* Éditions Thalita Koumi, mars 2013.

Laburthe-Tolra, Philippe et Bureau, René: *Initiation africaine: Supplément de philosophie et de sociologie à l'usage de l'Afrique noire,* Éditions CLÉ, Yaoundé, 1971.

Paul, Lucas: *The Pocket Book of Success, Inspiration to Achieve Your Goals,* Arcturus Publishing Limited, Copyright @ Arcturus Holdings Limited, London, 2015.

MacArthur, John (Pastor): *God's Design for a Successful Woman* (audio series), Grace Community Church in Sun Valley, California, Grace To You (gty.org), May 10, 2013.

Mbala Meka, Élise: *Le jour où il m'a dit "Je t'aime," il était déjà trop tard* (Roman), Les Éditions du Schabel, mars 2012.

Mbiti, John S.: *Introduction to African Region,* East African Educational Publishers, Nairobi/Kampala, 2nd Edition, 1992.

Megan Marshall, G. P. Putnam's Sons: *The Cost of Loving, Women and the New Fear of Intimacy,* New York, Copyright©1984.

Melone, Stanislas: *La parenté et la terre dans la stratégie du développement. L'expérience camerounaise: étude critique,* Yaoundé, Université fédérale du Cameroun, Paris, Klinesieck, 1972.

Menrad, Patrick: *La vie quotidienne en Afrique noire à travers la littérature africaine d'expression française*, l'Harmattan, Paris 1984.

Mintzer, Rich & Kathi: *The Everything Money Book, Learn How To Manage, Budget, Save, and Invest Your Money So There's Plenty Left Over,* Adam Media Corporation, Holbrook, Mssachussetts, Copyright©1999.

Mulago, Gwa Cikala: *La religion traditionnelle des Bantu et leur vision du monde,* Collection Bibliothèque du Centre d'Études des Régions Africaines: Faculté de Théologie Catholique, 2e édition, revue et corrigée, Kinshasa, 1980.

Ndongmo, Marcus: *Sauver la famille africaine, réflexions sur le mariage comme fondement de la famille*. Précis de la morale sexuelle et familiale, Presses de l'Université catholique de l'Afrique centrale (UCACA), Yaoundé, 2008.

Nicol, Yves: *La tribu des Bakoko,* Librairie coloniale et orientaliste Larose, Paris, 1929.

Njami-Nwandi, Simon Bolivar (Pastor): “La femme du Pasteur” in *Traité de Déontologie Pastorale*, Éditions Clé, Yaoundé, 2005.

Nsahi, Jules N. (Pastor): *Brisez l'empire de l'envoûtement par des rapports sexuels et de la malédiction dans le mariage*, Éditions Thalita Koumi, mars 2013.

Omartian, Stormie: *The Power of a Praying Wife*, Harvest House Publishers, Oregon, USA.

Pondi, Jean-Emmanuel: *Harcèlement sexuel et déontologie en milieu universitaire*, Éditions Clé, Yaoundé, 2011.

Terkeurst, Lysa:

- *Le Bonheur du couple, pour elle*, Guide pratique, Éditions Empreinte Temps Présent pour la traduction française publiée en accord avec Focus on the Family, 2005.
- *Le Bonheur du couple, pour lui*, Guide pratique, Éditions Empreinte Temps Présent pour la traduction française publiée en accord avec Focus on the Family, 2005.

Tyree, Omar: *For the Love of Money,* Simon & Schuster Rockefeller Center, New York, Copyright©2000.

Ulimwengu, John Mususa: *Appelés à être saints,* Éditions École de David, Kinshasa, JMU, 2014

Ury, William: *Comment dire NON, savoir refuser sans offenser,* Nouveaux Horizons, Éditions du Seuil, 2006.

Vallès Dominique, Bernadette Meunier: *Séparation, les enfants d'abord, des conseils pratiques pour les parents qui se séparent,* Hachette Livre (Hachette Pratique), 2003.

Von der Linde, Boris; et Steinweg, Svea: *Psychologie au bureau, bien gérer ses relations de travail,* les Miniguides Ecolibris, Ixelles Publishing S.A., Belgique, 2010.

Warren, Neil Clark: *The Cohabitation Epidemy,* clinical psychologist, eHarmony Founder, 2011.

Warren, Rick (Pastor): *The Purpose Driven Life: What on Earth I am Here Fo*r? Published by Zodervan, 1997.

Watch Tower: *Les Jeunes s'interrogent, Réponses pratiques,* Watch Tower Bible and Tract Society of New York, International Bible Students Association, Brooklyn, New York, 1989.

Williams Ntiri, Daphne: *One Is Not a Woman, One Becomes: The African Woman in a Transitional Society,* university of Michigan, 1988.

What the Bible Says about Money, Bible Answers to Life Questions, by Barbour Publishing, Inc, Ohio, USA, 2008

Yinda, Hélène et Ka Mana: *Manifeste de la femme africaine,* Collections Foi et Action, Éditions CIPCRE, Cameroun, 2005.

Zanga Tsogo, Delphine: *Vie de femmes,* Éditions Clé, Yaoundé, Cameroun 2000.

Newspapers, Articles, Magazines, Interviews, Radio Programs

Rainey, Dennis and Barbara; Auterburn, Steve; Lepine, Bob: *Family Life Today, Focus on the Family Institute of Marriage.*

The nationally syndicated call-in radio and TV shows on how to overcome family challenges; http://www.newlife.com.

Awake: *Infidelity—Its Tragic Consequences,* April 22, 1999 (p. 3–12)

France-Dimanche, No. 2311: *La vie du couple, pourquoi devient-on infidèle même quand on aime toujours son conjoint.*

Graham, Jack (Pastor):

- A woman's choice, Series: *The Godly Woman,* radio broadcast, May 10, 2013; www.jackgraham.org
- *To help your marriage,* in Power Point Podcast (radio), May 2013.

Jake, T.D. (Pastor): *The Ten Commandments for Working in a Hostile Environment* (CD).

L'Effort Camerounais: *The Secrets of Happy Couples,* Special edition, Yaoundé, 2014

Le Patriarche Info: *Le mariage pour tous n'est pas un modèle africain,* Mœurs et Société, No. 015, 25–30 avril 2013 (p. 3).

Stanley, Charles (Pastor): *Advancing through Adversity, Growing Stronger through Trials,* In Touch Ministries, Atlanta, GAMay 2003.

APPENDIX
Biblical References

The Bible contains sixty-six books for a total of 30,000 verses. The sample used in this book to convey our message is limited to selected verses from the New King James version (NKJV).

Marriage

1. And the Lord God said, "It is not good that man should be alone; I will make him a helper comparable to him." (Genesis 1:18)

2. "Therefore a man shall leave his father and mother and be joined to his wife, and they shall become one flesh." (Genesis 2:24). Read also: Matthew 19:5–6; Mark10:9; Mark 8:7–8; 1 Corinthians 7: 1–2; 1 Co 11:11–12.

3. "Then God blessed them, and God said to them, "Be fruitful and multiply; fill the earth and subdue it; have dominion over the fish of the sea, over the birds of the air, and over every living thing that moves on the earth." (Genesis 1:28).

4. "Wives, submit to your own husbands, as to the Lord. For the husband is head of the wife, as also Christ is head of the church; and He is the Savior of the body. Therefore, just as the church is subject to Christ, so let the wives be to their own husbands in everything. Husbands, love your wives, just as Christ also loved the church and gave Himself for her." (Ephesians 5:22–25). Read also1 Corinthians 11:3; 1 Peter 3:1.

5. "So husbands ought to love their own wives as their own bodies; he who loves his wife loves himself. For no one ever hated his own flesh, but nourishes and cherishes it, just as the Lord does the church." (Ephesians 28-29). Read also 1 Corinthians 11: 3; 1 Peter 3: 1.

6. "Let the husband render to his wife the affection due her, and likewise also the wife to her husband." (1 Corinthians 7:3).

7. "The wife does not have authority over her own body, but the husband does. And likewise the husband does not have authority over his own body, but the wife does." (1 Corinthians 7:4).

8. "Do not deprive one another except with consent for a time, that you may give yourselves to fasting and prayer; and come together again so that Satan does not tempt you because of your lack of self-control." (1 Corinthians 7:5). Read also 1 Corinthians 11:8–10.

9. "And though I have the gift of prophecy, and understand all mysteries and all knowledge, and though I have all faith, so that I could remove mountains, but have not love, I am nothing. And though I bestow all my goods to feed the poor, and though I give my body to be burned, but have not love, it profits me nothing. Love suffers long and is kind; love does not envy; love does not parade itself, is not puffed up; does not behave rudely, does not seek its own, is not provoked, thinks no evil; does not rejoice in iniquity, but rejoices in the truth; bears all things, believes all things, hopes all things, endures all things." (1 Corinthians 13:2–7).

10. "An excellent wife is the crown of her husband, but she who causes shame is like rottenness in his bones." (Proverbs 12:4).

11. Who can find a virtuous wife? For her worth is far above rubies. The heart of her husband safely trusts her; so he will have no lack of gain. She does him good and not evil all the days of her life." (Proverbs 31:10–12).

12. "Do not let your adornment be merely outward—arranging the hair, wearing gold, or putting on fine apparel— 4 rather let it be the hidden person of the heart, with the incorruptible beauty of a gentle and quiet spirit, which is very precious in the sight of God." (1 Peter 3:3–4). Read also: 1 Timothy 3:9.

13. "The wise woman builds her house, but the foolish pulls it down with her hands." (Proverbs 14:1).

14. "A bishop then must be blameless, the husband of one wife, temperate, sober-minded, of good behavior, hospitable, able to teach; 3 not given to wine, not violent, not greedy for money, but gentle, not quarrelsome, not covetous; 4 one who rules his own house well, having his children in submission with all reverence."

(1 Timothy 3:2–4). Read also: 1 Timothy 3:8–9, 12–13. These verses also apply to any respectable husband.

15. "Do not be unequally yoked together with unbelievers. For what fellowship has righteousness with lawlessness? And what communion has light with darkness? 15 And what accord has Christ with Belial? Or what part has a believer with an unbeliever?" (2 Corinthians 6:14–15).

16. "When you make a vow to God, do not delay to pay it; for He has no pleasure in fools. Pay what you have vowed" (Ecclesiastes 5:4).

17. "It is a snare for a man to devote rashly something as holy, and afterward to reconsider his vows." (Proverbs 20:25).

Adultery

18. "You shall not commit adultery" (Exodus 20:14). Read also: Deuteronomy 5:18.

19. "You have heard that it was said to those of old, 'You shall not commit adultery.' But I say to you that whoever looks at a woman to lust for her has already committed adultery with her in his heart." (Matthew 5:27–28).

20. "And I say to you, whoever divorces his wife, except for sexual immorality,[a] and marries another, commits adultery; and whoever marries her who is divorced commits adultery" (Matthew 19:9).

21. "So He said to them, "Whoever divorces his wife and marries another commits adultery against her. 12 And if a woman divorces her husband and marries another, she commits adultery." (Mark 10:11–12).

22. "The man who commits adultery with another man's wife, he who commits adultery with his neighbor's wife, the adulterer and the adulteress, shall surely be put to death." (Leviticus 20:10).

23. "Marriage is honorable among all, and the bed undefiled; but fornicators and adulterers God will judge." (Hebrews 13:4).

24. "Do you not know that your bodies are members of Christ? Shall I then take the members of Christ and make them members of a harlot? Certainly not!" (1 Corinthians 6:15).

25. "Flee sexual immorality. Every sin that a man does is outside the body, but he who commits sexual immorality sins against his own body." (1 Corinthians 6:18). Read also 1 Peter 2:11.

26. "Or do you not know that your body is the temple of the Holy Spirit who is in you, whom you have from God, and you are not your own? For you were bought at a price; therefore glorify God in your body and in your spirit, which are God's." (1 Corinthians 6:19–20). Read also: Proverbs 5:18–20; Matthew 6:22–23; Genesis 5:29.

27. "If your right eye causes you to sin, pluck it out and cast it from you; for it is more profitable for you that one of your members perish, than for your whole body to be cast into hell." (Matthew 5:29).

Divorce

28. "For the Lord God of Israel says That He hates." (Malachi 2:16).

30. "When a man takes a wife and marries her, and it happens that she finds no favor in his eyes because he has found some uncleanness in her, and he writes her a certificate of divorce, puts it in her hand, and sends her out of his house." (Deuteronomy 24:1).

31. "He said to them, "Moses, because of the hardness of your hearts, permitted you to divorce your wives, but from the beginning it was not so. And I say to you, whoever divorces his wife, except for sexual immorality, and marries another, commits adultery; and whoever marries her who is divorced commits adultery." (Matthew 19:8–9). Read also: 1 Corinthians 7:12–16.

32. "But even if she does depart, let her remain unmarried or be reconciled to her husband. And a husband is not to divorce his wife." (1 Corinthians 7:11).

33. "But if the unbeliever departs, let him depart; a brother or a sister is not under bondage in such cases. But God has called us to peace." (1 Corinthians 7:15).

34. "For this reason a man shall leave his father and mother and be joined to his wife, and the two shall become one flesh'? So then, they are no longer two but one flesh. Therefore what God has joined together, let not man separate." (Mathews 19:5–6). Read also Mark 10:9.

Remarriage

35. "Whoever divorces his wife and marries another commits adultery against her. And if a woman divorces her husband and marries another, she commits adultery." (Mark 10:11–12).

36. "A wife is bound by law as long as her husband lives; but if her husband dies, she is at liberty to be married to whom she wishes, only in the Lord. But she is happier if she remains as she is, according to my judgment—and I think I also have the Spirit of God." (1 Corinthians 7:39–40).

37. "When she has departed from his house, and goes and becomes another man's wife, 3 if the latter husband detests her and writes her a certificate of divorce, puts it in her hand, and sends her out of his house, or if the latter husband dies who took her as his wife, 4 then her former husband who divorced her must not take her back to be his wife after she has been defiled; for that is an abomination before the Lord, and you shall not bring sin on the land which the Lord your God is giving you as an inheritance." (Deuteronomy 24:2–4).

Celibacy

38. "For there are eunuchs who were born thus from their mother's womb, and there are eunuchs who were made eunuchs by men, and there are eunuchs who have made themselves eunuchs for the kingdom of heaven's sake. He who is able to accept it, let him accept it." (Matthew 19:12).

39. "But I say to the unmarried and to the widows: It is good for them if they remain even as I am; 9 but if they cannot exercise self-control, let them marry. For it is better to marry than to burn with passion." (1 Corinthians 7:8–9). Read also verses 27–28.

40. “But I want you to be without care. He who is unmarried cares for the things of the Lord—how he may please the Lord. But he who is married cares about the things of the world—how he may please his wife. There is a difference between a wife and a virgin. The unmarried woman cares about the things of the Lord, that she may be holy both in body and in spirit. But she who is married cares about the things of the world—how she may please her husband.” (1 Corinthians 7:32–34).

Monogamy

41. The following verses teach that monogamy is God’s standard: Genesis 2:18, 24; Malachi 2:14; Matthew 19:4–6; Mark 10:7–8, 11–12; 18:7–8; 1 Timothy 3:2–4, 8–9, 12–13; 1 Corinthians 7: 1–3, 11–12; Ephesians 5:22–33; 1 Pierre 3:1–5, etc.

The Spiritual and Eternal Marriage

42. “For your Maker is your husband, the Lord of hosts is His name; and your Redeemer is the Holy One of Israel; He is called the God of the whole earth. For the Lord has called you like a

woman forsaken and grieved in spirit, like a youthful wife when you were refused, Says your God." (Isaiah 54:5–6).

43. "And if I go and prepare a place for you, I will come again and receive you to Myself; that where I am, there you may be also."(John 14:3).

44. "Nor height nor depth, nor any other created thing, shall be able to separate us from the love of God which is in Christ Jesus our Lord." (Romans 8:39). Read also Revelation 19:9.

Homosexuality

45. "Nor shall you mate with any animal, to defile yourself with it. Nor shall any woman stand before an animal to mate with it. It is perversion." (Leviticus 18: 23)

46. "If a man lies with a male as he lies with a woman, both of them have committed an abomination. They shall surely be put to death. Their blood shall be upon them." (Leviticus 20:13).

47. "For this reason God gave them up to vile passions. For even their women exchanged the natural use for what is against nature. 27 Likewise also the men, leaving the natural use of the woman, burned in their lust for one another, men with men committing what is shameful, and receiving in themselves the penalty of their error which was due." (Romans 1:26–27).

CPSIA information can be obtained
at www.ICGtesting.com
Printed in the USA
FSOW02n0807211116
27521FS

9 781498 468022